Tales from the Trance

The Strange, the Sad, and the Solvable

D1602533

by
Jill Thomas, CHT

For permission, serialization, condensation, adaptions, or for our catalog of other publications, write to Ozark Mountain Publishing, Inc., P.O. Box 754, Huntsville, AR 72740, ATTN: Permissions Department.

Library of Congress Cataloging-in-Publication Data

Thomas, Jill – 1973 -
Tales from the Trance by Jill Thomas

You can't really get the whole picture of what is going on in life when you are standing too close and only looking at one aspect of it.

1. Metaphysical 2. Hypnosis   3. Healing 4. Past-lives
I. Jill Thomas, 1973 - II. Metaphysical III. Hypnosis IV. Title

Library of Congress Catalog Card Number: 2018963242
ISBN: 9781940265575

Cover Art and Layout: www.vril8.com
Book set in: Times New Roman, Maiandra GD
Book Design: Tab Pillar
Published by:

OZARK
MOUNTAIN
PUBLISHING

PO Box 754, Huntsville, AR 72740
800-935-0045 or 479-738-2348; fax 479-738-2448

WWW.OZARKMT.COM

Printed in the United States of America

Disclaimer

"The information provided to you is for general informational purposes only and is not intended or implied to serve as medical or therapeutic advice, diagnosis or treatment. You should not use the information in this book to diagnose or treat any health issues, illnesses or diseases. Jill Thomas is not providing any medical or therapeutic advice. If you have or suspect you have a health or therapeutic problem, you should consult with your doctor or therapist."

Contents

Chapter 1: Confessions of a Hypnotherapist   1

Chapter 2: The Hurdles of a Hypnotherapist   6

Chapter 3: The Life Half-Lived: Fears and Phobias   14

Chapter 4: Fun with Past-Lives Regressions   33

Chapter 5: Relationships … Another Word for Stress   45

Chapter 6: Fat Shaming Is Not a Weight-Loss Plan   73

Chapter 7: Teens—Smarter Than We Think   89

Chapter 8: Steering Clear of Judgment (Isn't Always Easy)   103

Chapter 9: Confidence   119

Chapter 10: Secondary Gain: Problems with a Purpose   135

Chapter 11: Anxiety: The Mother of All Symptoms   145

Chapter 12: Fails and Epic Fails   160

Chapter 13: It's Always about Healing   164

Chapter 14: Odds and Ends   170

Acknowledgments   196

About the Author   197

Chapter 1
Confessions of a Hypnotherapist

Standing in front of a room-sized Jackson Pollock painting on exhibition at the Getty Museum in Los Angeles, I realized I just didn't "get" the meaning of this work, which seemed like just a bunch of random paint and paper. Suddenly I heard a security guard say to me, "Ma'am, you're standing too close. You need to step back." Thinking he was trying to keep me from putting my hand on the priceless work of art, I apologized and retreated. He picked up on my reaction and quickly added, "No, that's not what I meant. It's just that you can't really see it from that close. It will never make sense if all you can see is that one small part. Come here… I'll show you."

The security guard/would-be philosopher had me go to the back of the room, where I could take in the entire painting at once. "See? From here it makes more sense," he said. "You can kind of see what he was trying to express." Although I still felt I was missing something with this particular Pollock work, I was struck with the larger idea he had demonstrated to me. *You can't really get the whole picture of what is going on in life when you are standing too close and only looking at one aspect of it.*

Like stepping back, modalities such as hypnotherapy, counseling, psychotherapy, and coaching help people see a bigger picture when they are too close to and involved in an issue or difficulty. Practitioners offer a new set of eyes as unbiased parties who can evaluate situations objectively and put them into more realistic proportions. By doing this, they can help direct your gaze from the weeds in your life to the amazing flowers blooming. An effective therapist is someone who believes in your ability to have the life you want, even when you don't see how this is possible from where you are now. In fact, they have likely seen resolution of problems far worse than yours, so they know it's possible in spite of your doubt and despair.

Working with a practitioner of some kind provides you a sounding board to be honest about the things you have done, including those you aren't proud of, without fear of being judged.

This is why I was drawn to hypnotherapy—I enjoy helping people get a different outlook and clearer understanding of their difficulties. More significantly, I love people! I love their quirks and the sometimes "weird" ways they view the world. Each person brings their own unique perspective to the table. Even if I entirely disagree with someone's point of view, each person lets me see the world through their eyes for just that short time we're together in session, and as a result, I am able to view the entire world a little differently from then on.

Although I'm passionate about healing, the thing I love most is listening to peoples' stories. When clients share honestly with me, I get to see behind the mask of what they want the world to know about them, a dynamic space where they reveal who they truly are. Most of us automatically exercise what my sociology teacher in college called "impression management." The clothes we wear, the stories we tell, the way we present ourselves to the world, and even our occupations reflect the person we want others to think we are. Often, this is just superficial camouflage hiding a less attractive reality, like pretending we have a perfect marriage when we don't, or driving an expensive car so it looks like we are doing well financially, when in actuality we are not.

I have worked with clients who belong to Alcoholics Anonymous (AA), and what I hear from them time and again is how much they love to hear gut-level honesty from others. Most of us have few opportunities to share like that in a place where we feel safe. But when we drop the mask, something beautiful and special happens— people become vulnerable enough to experience insight and change. I feel so privileged to witness this process!

In this book, honesty and perspective are what I hope to share by giving you full access to what goes on during hypnotherapy sessions. In the stories that follow, I open the doors of my office and give you a glimpse of what it's really like… what *people* are really like. Once you read details about all the things that trouble and puzzle others, you'll probably feel reassured about the issues that bother *you*. What you judge about yourself as so "strange" and "bad" may be more common than you think.

By gaining insight into the assortment of issues, challenges, and attitudes clients bring into my office every day, my hope is that people will be less afraid to seek help for themselves if they need it. Entertainment is a factor, too, but it goes deeper than that. Readers will be amused and captivated by the stories of some patients who seem like mental and/or emotional train wrecks, but besides feeling relieved about their own situations, will see that we all are not so different from one another, and it's unfair to judge situations and people we don't understand.

Above all, I hope to convey what I have learned from my clients about life and the meaning of being human. People are truly amazing … even those who seem ordinary. Human life is precious, particularly because of our capacity for love, whether it is love of self, love of family, or love of life in general.

Many of us need help to uncover that love, starting with finding it for ourselves and then spreading it outward to others and the world. I think most therapists would agree, at the end of the day, that healing really is all about love.

My Prime Directives

There are a few basic rules that I have developed and put into place over time. These rules promote the best relationship possible between me and my clients. I call them my "prime directives," which should really be "primary objectives," I suppose, except that I'm a Star Trek die-hard, and if they're good enough for the United Federation of Planets, they're good enough for my hypnotherapy practice! These are:

- Let people tell their stories without judging them
- Always assume the person talking to you is completely serious
- Know who is—and who isn't—your client
- Remember that this work is all about love

<u>Let people tell their stories without judging them</u>:

Although these basics seem obvious and like they should be easy to do, I can tell you from experience that it's *not* always easy to remain detached when the person in front of you is sharing certain things, especially when it's some dreadful, immoral thing they have done.

<u>Always assume that the person talking to you is completely serious</u>:

Sometimes, people will call about something that sounds completely bizarre, and I have to remind myself to assume that everyone is serious. That is, unless the caller is giggling and sounds like my brother.

<u>Know who is—and who isn't—your client</u>:

For me, especially in the beginning when I was somewhat desperate for business, I wasn't yet able to recognize people who had problems that weren't appropriately dealt with through hypnotherapy. There are those who need more intensive help or a different type of help than I can offer. Learning the types of issues I could and couldn't address came with time and experience, and it was important for both me and the prospective client to be sensitive to this.

<u>Remember that this work is all about love</u>:

Last, but most important, this work is about love. Sometimes, working from a place of love means saying "no" to late-night appointments when I know I won't be at my best. Setting boundaries and rules with clients helps both of us feel comfortable with the process. Offering my services with a foundation of love means that first and foremost, I encourage all my clients to become aware of their individual importance to the world. Sometimes I admit I fail, which you will see in the section of this book called "Fails and Epic Fails," but I always give it my very best.

Who Is a Good Candidate for Hypnotherapy?

For the most part, my clients are basically mentally healthy individuals who are trying to make a change that they haven't been able to accomplish on their own; for example, lose weight, quit smoking, or stop some other bad habit. Other people who can be helped through hypnotherapy are people who respond to life's stressors with feelings of anxiety, fear, or low confidence. All of these responses, however, are on some level habit-based behaviors. In other words, everyone's life includes stress, but how a person responds to it can be habit based.

Others whom I help want something in life, but find themselves doing things to sabotage their success. Examples would be dating the same dysfunctional person over and over again, not asking for what they need, not taking risks, or allowing feelings of fear to keep them from doing the things they need to do in order to succeed. All of these issues are solvable through hypnotherapy.

Chapter 2
The Hurdles of a Hypnotherapist

What a Hypnotherapist Is up Against

One day, my husband came home from work and told me about a conversation he'd had with a new coworker who had asked him what his wife did for a living. When my husband told him I was a hypnotherapist, the coworker asked the same question I get just about every time I mention my career: "Does that really work?" He'd answered, "I'm pretty sure it does. She's a very popular hypnotherapist." His coworker joked, "Has she ever hypnotized you to get you to take out the trash?" then answered himself, "No, she hasn't—that you know of…" My husband laughed and told him that first, that's not how hypnosis works, and second, if I ever wanted him to take out the trash, I would just ask. No tricks necessary.

This was a taste of the many misconceptions people have about hypnosis. Besides causing me to get a lot of strange and tricky phone calls, the mistaken ideas people have about hypnosis frustrate me, because people who could really benefit from hypnotherapy are not getting that help due to not understanding what it actually is. Unfortunately, TV is not doing the hypnotherapy community any favors with its inaccurate portrayal of the process.

How TV Gets Hypnosis Wrong!

I watched an episode of *Elementary* (not a great show, by the way; watch *Sherlock* instead), in which someone claimed to not remember committing a crime that the evidence had clearly shown they committed. I started thinking, *Oh, please, don't try to say someone hypnotized that person into committing this crime. That is too stupid and cliché.* Sure enough, this exact inaccurate and overused plot line followed, leaving me yelling at the TV about how stupid and wrong this was, while my husband laughed.

Hollywood loves to paint hypnosis as nefarious because it makes for an interesting plot twist, while standard talk-it-out therapy is always painted in a beneficial, almost angelic light. What people don't see is that talk therapy, even though it does work, takes quite a bit of time. Hypnotherapy, although not a fit for every issue, brings results much faster.

Even one of my favorite TV shows, *True Blood*, had vampires using some kind of hypnosis to make people do things. I kept waiting for one of those vampires to open an office with a big sign saying, "Quit smoking today!" but it never happened. I have also seen a bunch of silly movies where they showed hypnotized people doing things they normally wouldn't do. Usually the character does something really evil or just ridiculous, as in the case of *The Incredible Burt Wonderstone* (a seriously bad movie), in which a whole audience was hypnotized and then moved to a new location. Even *Office Space*, although funny as heck, had the main character doing some crazy things after seeing a hypnotherapist and getting "stuck" in a hypnotic state (which is not possible, by the way).

This bothers me because it keeps people who need help from seeking it, out of fear someone will implant some crazy idea into their head, and they will kill their mother and not remember it! Using hypnosis, you cannot make someone do anything they don't want to do. In fact, sometimes you can't even make them do something they *want* to do. If they do it, it is done by and for themselves. Some people, however, are more successful with hypnotherapy than others because they are more open to change.

Don't believe what you see on TV about hypnosis. Remember that even the news has become "entertainment," and most of the time, the truth is not really that amusing without a little help from a good writer.

What Is Hypnosis, Anyway?

The short definition of hypnosis is that it's a very relaxed state of mind, somewhere between sleep and wakefulness, which allows access to the unconscious mind. It is there, in the unconscious part of our mind, that beliefs are stored and habits and some decisions are generated.

While in the hypnotic state, you feel very physically relaxed and yet more alert than normal. You are better able to concentrate and more open to suggestions than in your usual waking state.

Most people don't realize this, but a typical person hypnotizes themselves all the time. When you are focusing on something so intently that the whole world fades away and you lose track of time and space, this is actually a light state of hypnosis. This relaxed state allows the mind to absorb information and learn something new.

Scientists and engineers do this all the time as part of their job, which is why as clients they frequently are the first ones to come out of trance and say they weren't hypnotized because they didn't feel any different from how they feel all day long. Of course, by coincidence, they stop smoking the day of their session, but they still question whether they were hypnotized. Grrrrr…

Hypnosis vs. Meditation

Some hypnotherapists use the terms *hypnosis* and *meditation* interchangeably because basically, a "guided meditation" is a hypnotic session. It might not be as deep as a hypnosis session with a practitioner, but essentially, it's the same. One of my teachers told us that sometimes, people will call and say that because of either their religious beliefs or fear, they don't want to do "hypnosis." He told us to just respond to them, "That's okay. We will do guided imagery instead." Then, during the session, he advised, simply do the same thing you would with hypnosis.

The line between waking consciousness and hypnosis is really based on what state the brain waves are in. Brain-wave cycles basically fall into one of four levels, based on cycles per second:

- *Beta*: Normal waking consciousness.
- *Alpha*: A relaxed state. If you are really focused on this book right now, you might be in this state. You experience alpha brain-wave activity twice every day—while drifting

off to sleep and waking up from sleep. It constitutes a light to medium level of hypnosis.
- *Theta*: Early stages of sleep. This is a medium to deep level of hypnosis.
- *Delta*: Deep sleep. This is the state in which you dream.

Deeper Is Not Always Better

Some clients who've done a little reading beforehand come to me saying they want me to bring them to a deep level of hypnosis before we do any therapy. However, deeper is not necessarily better. A light state of hypnosis is still very effective, and for some things—like processes where I need the person to be able to answer questions for me—I don't want them to be at a deeper level. There are some issues better addressed in a deep trance, but ideally, I work with clients in both levels. If the hypnotic state is too deep, I run the risk of putting a client to sleep. Even this could still work, but the person might not remember what we talked about.

How Is It Done?

Therapeutic hypnosis is most commonly done by having the subject close their eyes, and then directing them to think about certain things that will help them get into a relaxed state. With the unconscious mind more receptive in this state, the practitioner guides the subject to begin looking at the presenting problem in a different way. There are other techniques, but this is the one most commonly used.

The unconscious mind does not know the difference between a real and an imagined event. This is the reason why, when you have a dream that your grandmother is chasing you with a knife, you wake up really scared, even though the reality is that your grandmother most likely doesn't want you dead (and you could easily outrun her if she did!). With hypnosis, we use that quality of the unconscious mind to create a world where dogs are good, cigarettes are bad, and nothing stresses you out. In this way, you can release fears that aren't helping you and habits that will eventually kill you if you don't stop them.

If you have a habit or issue, such as a specific fear, which is interfering with your life, it is very likely that you're not consciously aware of its basis. For instance, a dog bite that happened to a young child—which by the way, the child might easily remember—can result in a belief that a certain type of dog is dangerous, or even worse, that all dogs are dangerous. This child grows into an adult, but still can't get past the fear of dogs.

Stage Shows vs. Therapeutic Hypnotherapy

For most of my prospective clients, their only experience witnessing hypnosis live will have been an entertainment stage show at a local fair or in Las Vegas, where they make people do weird things such as bark like a dog, think they are on fire and start running, or any number of other amusingly bizarre stunts.

As a hypnotherapist who practices near one of the biggest county fairs in the country, I both love and hate these shows. I love them because as a result of them, people know about hypnosis. However, the shows have it wrong when it comes to therapeutic hypnosis. People come away from these performances thinking hypnosis is mind control, making them afraid and fascinated at the same time. Clients have said things to me such as, "I saw how that hypnotist made a man on stage crack a broom swatting at a spider that wasn't there, so I thought maybe it could make me stop eating chocolate." Well, yes and no.

This comes up a lot with prospective patients, especially the more scientifically minded people who tell me they are afraid they can't be hypnotized because they are certain the techniques used in stage hypnosis won't work on them. I assure them they are correct, that the techniques wouldn't work on them or anyone who doesn't really want to get up there and do those crazy things. Stage hypnotists are entertainers, remember, and have taken classes on how to carefully select the people they bring on stage, including weeding out those who are not good candidates. One example of the dramatic effect is how stage hypnotists often play up the action of taking their glasses off and putting them on, making it seem as though their eyes are hypnotizing the participants. It's all part of the show, and it *is* a show.

Real therapeutic hypnosis is done very differently, and as I jokingly tell people, "It's really not nearly that interesting."

On the other hand, just because you wouldn't be one of those people chosen to be part of a show doesn't mean you can't be hypnotized. I have had several calls from people who were initially picked, then sent off the stage because they weren't hypnotized enough for the entertainer's approval. These people tell me they are afraid they can't be hypnotized because they didn't go under enough while on stage, in front of several hundred people. When that comes up, I assure them this is not the case. Even I, who am easily hypnotized and trying as hard as I can, would never be able to be in a deep enough trance to do the idiotic stuff I've seen on stage, because as a natural introvert, I would never want to. Being a good stage show participant is not as much about one's ability to be hypnotized as much as the desire to perform in front of a lot of people.

For the most part, stage techniques are meant to be temporary. It's just for the audience—entertainment—and quite different altogether from hypnosis used for therapy. You'll never see someone under hypnosis on stage say, "I was raped as a teenager, and now I am afraid of men in general. Can you fix that?" There's far too much reality in that to be entertaining!

Although I get annoyed having to answer questions like, "Are you going to make me bark like a dog?" from a new client, I am grateful that stage entertainers are spokespeople who are able to expose great numbers of people to the concept of hypnosis, even if they portray it inaccurately.

Can Anyone Be Hypnotized?

This is a question I'm asked often, probably because where I practice in San Diego, there is a high concentration of technology companies. This makes many clients who are scientists and engineers. As technically inclined individuals, many of them question the effectiveness of a process they see as somewhat "mystical," mistakenly associating being able to be easily hypnotized with being gullible. The truth is, the more intelligent and imaginative the person, the more easily he or she can be hypnotized. And just as an intelligent person wouldn't fall for a sketchy sales pitch, they would not do the bizarre things people do on stage. This certainly doesn't mean the smart person can't be hypnotized—again, the opposite is true. Personally, I love working with scientists and engineers. This may be because I am somewhat scientific myself. At any rate, I find them easy to hypnotize.

Admittedly, I use slightly different processes on artistic types than I use on scientists. The artist will tell you that they see everything I describe during hypnosis in graphic detail, while the scientist may only have seen one small portion of the suggested imagery. Both people were hypnotized, but their minds don't process things the same way. This doesn't negate the fact that both types of people can experience profound results from hypnotherapy.

One type of phone call I get that does frustrate me as a professional is when some obviously bright person has already gone to another hypnotherapist, typically a brand-new practitioner, didn't get the results they were hoping for, complained to the hypnotherapist, and were told that they couldn't be hypnotized. This is total nonsense!

I hope through this discussion that I've communicated the bottom line: hypnosis is safe, effective, really fun, and can bring about deep and lasting change for the better! I encourage everyone to give it a try at some point. Who knows? It might just change your life.

One Last Thing...

So... ready to dive in and learn what it's really like to be a hypnotherapist? Great! Let's get started! But first, a few words of disclosure.

None of the names in the following chapters are real, although the stories are. Some accounts are a combination of several clients' stories, certain details have been altered for privacy, and some ideas are relayed as client experiences, but may be my own. (I am a practitioner, but I am also someone's client.) If you are one of the people I have worked with and something sounds like your situation, know that after seeing hundreds of clients, I've heard a thousand versions of the same story by now. I can assure you that in spite of how you see your own challenges, people have universally similar experiences. The details may change, but the core content is basically the same.

Furthermore, you may disagree with the advice I gave the clients I write about here, which is obviously your right. I will say, as I gain more insight about particular problems, that even I develop new approaches on how to best promote healing. Certainly, I don't claim to be perfect, and sometimes things go a bit sideways in spite of my best efforts; however, I do endeavor on a daily basis to bring healing to my clients, so they are better equipped to create the life they want for themselves. And so the journey begins...

Chapter 3
The Life Half-Lived: Fears and Phobias

Be Not Afraid

Not surprisingly, many of my clients are people plagued by fears and phobias. I greatly admire the people who actually seek help, because it is much easier to let fear ground you than it is to face it and do something about it. Sadly, I have known too many people, both personally and professionally, who hide behind fear as an excuse for what is often a life half-lived.

In some ways, an acute fear that you are exposed to all the time, such as fear of driving or of leaving the house (agoraphobia), can be a bit like having a drug addiction. Once triggered by some event—for example, finding out about an out-of-state trade show that one is required to attend—the person with the fear begins to spend an extraordinary amount of time thinking about it. They may try to psych themselves up for it, worry about how they're going to control their anxiety (which adds to the first fear, bringing them closer to panic), and try to figure out ways to avoid the situation. Huge amounts of time and emotional energy are used up fretting... energy that could be directed to more productive things, such as preparing for the event or even better, getting help for the problem of excessive fear.

Fear Affects Your Loved Ones

Fear can be devastating to both the life of the person experiencing it and those around them. This is especially true in the case of fears like driving (subcategories might include driving on the freeway, driving over bridges, or driving at night) and flying. Not only is the fearful individual dependent on others to help manage that issue, but it prevents them from enjoying some of life's most amazing experiences with the ones they love. For instance, not many people would leave their phobic spouse at home and take the rest of the family on a spectacular trip to Disneyland or the Grand Canyon, so everyone in the family winds up missing out. Or how can you plan a mother/daughter spa day if mom is afraid to take the freeway needed to get to the day spa? An opportunity for mother/daughter bonding is lost.

Sometimes a family may try to accommodate the person with a fear of flying by driving somewhere instead. This could work, but the trip might take on a different tone entirely if family members are trapped together in a car for a twenty-hour road trip (I'm still trying to get over the trauma of a couple of these trips myself). Resentment toward the family member who can't shed his or her fear is a frequent consequence of unaddressed phobias. Not only do the family members feel like they can't enjoy "normal" family activities, but the person with the excessive fear feels isolated by the limitations their terror imposes.

The following are the most common fears I see in my office:

Fear of flying:

Somewhat seasonal, this particular fear pops up more often when the holidays are approaching. However, it is a common issue that I address with many clients all year round. At the root of this problem is fear of losing control. Think about it—once the plane doors close, we are completely under someone else's power. Passengers can't even use the restroom until indicated, and certainly can't step outside for some fresh air. It is actually rare to see a client whose issue with flying was caused by a real, traumatic experience on a plane, other than having an onboard panic attack from feeling trapped.

Fear of driving on the freeway:

Some of my colleagues who live in less-populated areas tell me this fear isn't one they encounter in many clients, but here in Southern California, our freeways are big and wide, fast, with overpasses that are as high as roller coasters in some places, not to mention the people pulling some outrageous driving maneuvers. Add to this the occasional earthquake that takes out a portion of an overpass or entire freeway, like the Nimitz freeway collapse in 1989 during the Loma Prieta earthquake, documented by hours of graphic television news coverage, and it's easy to see why people develop "freeway fear."

Fear of throwing up:

This fear may seem surprising—at least, I used to think so—but being afraid to vomit actually has presented itself fairly frequently in my practice. Usually, the underlying cause is related to fear of losing control or looking bad in front of others. Interestingly enough, this fear is the most common one among the teenagers I work with. Fear of public speaking is another typical teen fear, but anxiety about throwing up is much more prevalent.

Fear of acute illness or dying:

In nine out of ten patients who come to me for help with this fear, the person either grew up with a family member in their household suffering a long-term illness that ended in death—often a parent with cancer—or witnessed a family member having a major, debilitating injury that altered their family life forever. Typically, the clients with this fear are the most physically healthy of anyone I work with, but at the least sign of a health issue, like a strange bump or sudden twinge anywhere on their body, they become terrified and run to the doctor, convinced they are dying of some awful disease. I feel tremendous compassion for people with this obsessive apprehension… it's a difficult way to live, to say the least.

Fear of public speaking:

Here it is, the old standby. Although a very common fear I see in my clients, it is not as frequent as the others discussed previously. Most of the clients who come to me regarding this issue are scientists and engineers who have to give short status updates on their projects. Many of these people, who are mostly males, have had very little experience with public speaking and are vastly uncomfortable with it.

Something I have noticed about fears over my years in practice is that they often seem to be a "gift" from parents or grandparents. I don't mean that excessive fears are genetic, although I suppose this could be a factor. Rather, I think a child observes the reactions and attitudes of their parents and other family members to a situation or object, and on some level concludes that it must be dangerous. Remember that to a child, mom and dad are the center of the universe, and if they are afraid of something, it surely *must* be bad.

I have also observed that these tendencies children learn from their parents often sit and wait, like a ticking time bomb, until some point in adulthood. Frequently, clients tell me, "One day I was fine, but then [something—fill in the blank] happened, and after that I was afraid, just like my mom had been." It's sad to witness how this occurs, but it is very understandable and solvable, with help.

In terms of resolution, some of these fears are relatively quick to confront and overcome; for example, public speaking and flying. Others, such as fear of throwing up, are harder and take more work to resolve. Across the board, however, most people who seek help through hypnotherapy for fear problems see significant improvement in a fairly short amount of time.

"Help! I'm Afraid of Dying"

As mentioned before, the clients who want my help with an excessive fear of dying are, in general, some of the healthiest clients I see. They tend to pay attention to what they eat, work out regularly, have an interest in alternative medicine, and are often already familiar with or working in the healing arts. Nonetheless, people with a fear of dying have one of the saddest fears I see, because it often keeps them from truly living.

My client Miranda was no exception. A yoga teacher and nutrition counselor in her thirties, she stuck to a strictly vegan diet, didn't drink or use drugs, worked out regularly, and led what looked to me like one of the healthiest lifestyles I've seen.

When she came in and started to describe her debilitating fear of dying, I stopped her and asked, "Was it your mother or your father who died when you were a child?" Looking stunned, she replied, "My father. How did you know?" I explained that I see this circumstance all the time and have found it's usually the result of losing a parent or sibling to illness early in life.

In this client's case, her father had been diagnosed with lymphoma when she was five years old, and his slow decline and eventual death eight years later colored every aspect of her childhood. "We would be at a family event, and suddenly Dad would have some health crisis," she told me. "Then we would have to go to the hospital and he'd be there for several days. This happened all the time while I was growing up, and I always felt like at any moment, anything fun could quickly change to a crisis involving my dad's health. I learned not to get excited about family events, and stopped allowing myself to enjoy them.

"I feel guilty about this, but I used to really resent him because nothing in my childhood ever got to be about me. It was always about Dad and his illness. I was almost relieved when he died, because I thought I would at least get some attention again from my mom. That didn't happen, though. She spent the next two years grieving, and then got a new boyfriend whom she later married. After that, everything became about him and what she could do to make him happy. I felt robbed of a childhood.

"I am so afraid of getting sick and putting my kids through the same thing! Whenever I notice a new mole or freckle, or feel any sudden pain anywhere, even if it's minor, I become upset and scared, and convince myself I must have cancer and am going to die."

I asked Miranda which was scarier to her—dying or being sick? She thought about it and said, "You know, that's a good question. I think I'm more afraid of being sick, like my dad, and having my whole life be about cancer."

What this client told me was similar to what I hear frequently from other patients who grew up around serious illness in a parent or sibling. Besides the terror of dying or getting sick themselves, there are feelings of guilt and resentment. The person feels resentful toward the sick family member because that person's illness deprived them of a normal childhood, and then they are plagued by guilt for feeling this way. Another client put it best: "I feel awful for thinking this, but I was sad and yet glad when my brother died after being sick for so many years. I didn't have much of a childhood because of his illness, although I do miss him very much. Does that make me a bad person?"

The answer to this question is obviously "no." Those feelings are normal and should be acknowledged. I have often speculated that the fear of dying or sickness is, on some level, a way of punishing oneself out of guilt about what happened and the person's reaction, since the fear and guilt are so frequently and strongly linked. The sad thing is that in some ways, the fearful person already has the illness they so dread, because so much of their energy goes toward being afraid of it. If left unaddressed, the phobic person runs the risk of passing those same fears to their children.

This particular fear is one of the more difficult ones to treat, but healing is possible. Resolving the issue usually involves a combination of several approaches, including mourning the loss of the childhood the person would have desired, forgiving themselves for the resentment and other emotions related to what happened, and learning to have faith that just because something happened to someone close to them, it doesn't have to happen to them.

One sticking point in overcoming this problem is that for people whose childhood was so filled with health concerns, doctors, and treatments, there is an expectation on some level that their entire life will be the same way. These individuals need to practice trusting that everything will be okay and that if something is wrong, they will know early enough to do something about it. In the case of Miranda, she admitted that her mom had revealed to her that her dad had some very strange symptoms early on, but chose to ignore them because he was afraid of what they might indicate. As often happens, peoples' fear of a diagnosis keeps them from getting immediate treatment. Certainly, this is a mistake Miranda wouldn't make, with her bodily hypervigilance. She remarked to me, "If he had gone to the doctor early in his illness, he might still be with us today. And for that, I do have some resentment toward him."

Fear can be a good and useful feeling, warning us of genuine danger. But in the case of excessive fears and phobias, our brain's natural cautionary instinct has reached a counterproductive level that, like cancer, eats away at our health, freedom, and joy.

Dog Terror with a Twist

Many people choose to suffer with a fear of dogs rather than seek treatment. In so doing, however, they miss an opportunity to heal what is usually a different and deeper problem that affects other aspects of their life. I have found that usually, the issue for which a patient comes to me is actually just a symptom of something more fundamental. This is especially true for troubles with weight loss, anxiety, relationships, and specific fears—like the fear of dogs.

For example, a fear of flying and/or claustrophobia typically represents fear of losing control. A fear of earthquakes (in my California clients) is often rooted in fear of losing people one cares about. When you only address the symptom, as opposed to discovering and working on the core issue causing it—frequently the case in conventional psychotherapy and sometimes hypnotherapy—the underlying pain eventually returns in the form of a relapse to the presenting symptom or the appearance of some other difficulty.

Such was the case with Sally, who came in to address her fear of dogs. After one session, she saw improvement, because this particular fear is fairly easy to release. Sally told me she felt better, but that the treatment hadn't entirely removed her symptoms.

During another of our sessions, I decided to take her to a deeper level of hypnosis and then use a technique to regress to the original traumatic event, in hopes of releasing the charge on that issue. Sally had actually been bitten by a dog three times, at ages four, seven, and twenty-two. When I used the regression technique and asked her to tell me her age, she said she was seven. I didn't think we were back to the original event, which she had told me occurred at four years old. I repeated the suggestion to go back to the original event. While under hypnosis, however, she reiterated that she was at that event. I figured we'd just stay there.

I had her explain what happened, and this time, she gave more details than during our pre-session talk. Under hypnosis, Sally brushed quickly past the dog bite and the pain of the injury, and proceeded to spend a lot of time talking about the beating she received from her father after being bitten by the dog.

"He was angry at me because I defied him," Sally stated. "He said he told me not to pet the dog. Maybe he had, but I had an ear infection and didn't hear him. I didn't hear the dog growl either." Now I understood why our first session together didn't bring the issue to complete resolution. This conflict wasn't about the dog at all. It was about the violence perpetrated by her father while she was still bleeding from the dog bite. Her mind had tied the two events together and made it about the dog, causing her to feel afraid of all dogs.

I guided her through a healing process to release the fear, which included forgiving the dog for doing what dogs sometimes do, and then deciding what she wanted to do about her dad. Under hypnosis, she said she wanted to imagine that he wasn't even there. So, she took him out of the memory and rescued the little girl trapped in that memory to update and bring her into the present.

Sally came out of hypnosis feeling refreshed and a bit surprised by what she had recalled. "My father was abusive while I was growing up, and I remembered that beating and all the others over the years. But until now, I didn't realize how significant that particular incident had been."

I suggested we schedule another appointment for two weeks later, thinking we still needed to go back to the original dog bite, when she had been four years old. The next day, I got an amazing phone call from a very excited Sally, who told me a story I was not expecting.

"Jill, you won't believe this, but last night my dad called. Something bizarre happened. When the phone rang and I saw his number on the caller ID, I *didn't* tense up. The thing is, I didn't realize I did that every time he called until I suddenly wasn't doing it! The whole phone call felt a lot better than normal, too. I didn't feel so nervous talking to him, nor did I feel uncomfortable telling him 'no' when he asked me if we could get together this weekend. You see, it wasn't really the dog I was afraid of… it was my dad. After that last session, I realized I no longer feel afraid of my dad *or* dogs. Actually, my dad was the bigger problem, but I didn't realize that until now."

I was surprised and happy for her, although I knew there was more work we needed to do to heal the effects of her dad's physical and emotional abuse. At least now, though, we were working at the root of her problems rather than just chopping away at the branches. That would not have been the case if we had only focused on her initial symptom, fear of dogs.

More sessions addressing the core issue helped Sally heal permanently from an uneasiness that was affecting almost every area of her life, because her fear of her father had morphed into a fear and distrust of men in general. It really was a huge breakthrough for her and a catalyst for amazing positive changes to come.

Strong Marine, Scary Peacocks

I picked up an alarming voicemail message left by a man claiming he needed to schedule an emergency appointment. The word *emergency* always makes me nervous, because the person may be suicidal and contacting me thinking I'm a psychotherapist. You can imagine my relief when a young man answered the phone and told me he needed to schedule a rush appointment about a particular fear he had. When I asked what his fear was, I thought I'd heard him wrong.

"I'm sorry," I said. "Did you say 'peacocks'?" He had to be joking. But remembering my prime directive, I stifled the chuckle about to escape.

"Yes," he reiterated. "Peacocks. I hate those *stupid* peacocks. I'm afraid of them, and I need this handled by Saturday."

Okay, then. I told him, "I am sure I can see you before then… but out of curiosity, why Saturday?"

"Because I am going to the San Diego Zoo with a bunch of friends, and they have peacocks there," he replied. My first thought, "There are peacocks at the zoo?" He explained he was in the military and on leave with some of his buddies. Someone had zoo passes, so they planned to go. "I don't want to embarrass myself in front of them."

I have worked with clients who fear just about every barnyard animal that exists, and have heard many variations on the same basic animal angst. Geese are usually the offending animal, although I have heard quite a few stories about horses as well. This particular client, who was stationed at a local marine base, Camp Pendleton, was originally from Ohio. He'd grown up on a farm, and he hadn't gotten on well with the peacocks his family kept. Apparently, they had chased and pecked at him every time he was in the yard by himself.

When he'd been a small boy, the peacocks were bigger than he was. But although he'd grown taller, the fear had remained locked in his psyche. When they chase him now, this young man admitted, he often screams involuntarily. "That's fine when you're six years old," he went on, "but not so much when you're twenty-five and in the company of fellow marines."

For some reason, animals you are afraid of seem to know this, and will chase you no matter how old you are. It's like you are marked for abuse! It's the same kind of thing cats seem to know as they jump into the lap of the one houseguest who is allergic to them.

In this case, I worked with him to release his fear and let go of his embarrassing response to the animal. This young man's peacock reaction was as much a habit as his fear, and I hoped that at the very least, we could stop him from shrieking and fleeing at the sight of them.

Our session went well. I later received an e-mail from him saying he'd had a great time at the zoo, and for once, the peacocks left him alone. Several weeks later, I visited the zoo myself. While enjoying a cup of coffee at one of the cafés there, a group of peacocks strutted over, and one of them pecked my foot! I guess my client had been right… there are peacocks at the zoo, and they are mean. *Stupid* peacocks!

Needled with Fear

Sean was an elderly client seeking hypnotherapy to address his deathly fear of needles. With this particular fear, it has been my experience that it is almost always associated with fear of hospitals, doctors' offices, or anything related to medical care, so I asked him about these other possible aversions. He actually became a bit defensive at my questions, however, and kept saying, "No. I just want to focus on my fear of needles. Just that."

Sean also seemed nervous about the hypnosis process, which is understandable, and I spent a good deal of time reassuring him of its safety and therapeutic value. In spite of my explanations, however, he was still hesitant. Finally, feeling there was only so much explaining I could do, I suggested we simply move forward into the experience. Sean's reservations about the process were evident, and he wouldn't open up much during hypnotherapy. I did a somewhat generic technique targeted at fear of needles, but I had the sense he wasn't going to get the resolution he was hoping for.

As I predicted, he called later to say that our session had lessened his fear to some degree, and he wanted to come back and take another shot at it. Because he knew what to expect the second time around, he was more relaxed and open to what we were doing.

During the next session, Sean admitted it was more than a fear of needles. He was afraid of anything medical, especially hospitals. He further revealed that after a car accident he had been in, he'd refused an ambulance and instead asked a bystander to take him to the emergency room. (I could somewhat understand this, having once spent $2,000 on a ten-minute ride to the hospital myself.) Sean said his fear was so intense, he hadn't gone to the hospital to be with his wife when his daughters were born, much to her dismay. He later admitted, "I'm actually surprised our marriage survived that one." Me too, to be honest.

I explained to Sean that all of these fears were likely connected. We could spend a lot of time working on the surface issues one by one, or we could do some deeper work to get to the root cause. Fortunately, he agreed the latter made more sense.

C. Roy Hunter and Bruce Eimer, authors of *The Art of Hypnotic Regression Therapy: A Clinical Guide*, describe what they call the "initial sensitizing event" and the "activating event" in regressive hypnotherapy. These are a client's memories that bring them to my office for help, assuming that these specific events caused the problem. Frequently they can be the cause, but not always, as turned out to be the case with Sean.

When I asked him how or when this issue with needles started, Sean told me a story about a physical he'd been required to undergo prior to his enlistment as a soldier in World War II. During this physical, he'd been given several shots, which he believed had been various vaccinations. They had also drawn a lot of blood to run tests, and while they were doing that, he passed out. Even worse, when he passed out, he fell and hit his head on something, necessitating a trip to the hospital for stitches.

During hypnotherapy, we went through a process to clear the charge on this memory, and although this helped him again, it didn't take care of the problem entirely. I suspected an earlier, similar event was the root cause, so at the next session, I took him back to the initial sensitizing event related to his fear of anything medical.

Sean told me a story he had forgotten until then. When he was a young child living in Virginia, he'd had an uncle whom he really loved. His uncle had some type of medical problem that kept him from being able to get a job and move out of Sean's parents' home. Sean said, "I can't be sure, because no one would talk about it, but I think he had epilepsy. And because of that, he wasn't able to work very much." At one point, Sean reported, his family found it too difficult to take care of him, and some men came from the Trans-Allegheny Lunatic Asylum (subsequently the Weston State Hospital, which closed in 1994) and hauled his uncle off, "like he was a criminal." This happened right in front of Sean, and he never saw his uncle again. His uncle died a year later under mysterious circumstances, and Sean felt deeply saddened by the loss.

Because of the confusion and sadness he harbored around his beloved uncle being taken away forever, Sean developed a fear of going into the hospital and never coming out. He extended this feeling to distrusting the medical community in general.

While his fears might have been reasonable and well founded by the situation then, they were interfering with his life now. Under hypnosis, I guided Sean through a process where the adult self helps the inner child to see how things have changed, and show him that it was now safe to go to a hospital, where it was his choice to stay or leave.

This time the process worked completely, and my client was finally able to go to the doctor's office for a much-needed physical. The prognosis? A clean bill of health, which is very fortunate for an eighty-year-old. Sean's e-mail about his physical surprised me somewhat, though. He wrote, "After all that, I didn't even need to fix this problem. If my wife had just listened to me when I said I didn't need to go see the doctor, I wouldn't have had to spend the money to see you or fix this issue." I just had to laugh about his inability to see the value of solving a problem that had caused so many other problems in his life. So often people say it's about money and the cost of getting help. I equate it a bit more to love. They love or value their money more than they value themselves. A human being's life is so valuable and the ability to live it to the fullest so precious, I wonder why anyone would place the value of a relatively tiny amount of money ahead of that.

Intuition vs. Paranoia

Clients always ask me, "How do I know the difference between receiving an intuitive message versus feeling fear that has been activated?" What they mean is, how can one tell the difference between a real, "normal" fear, which as I mentioned before is one of our brain's beneficial ways of signaling danger, and an excessive or irrational fear?

Besides having extensive professional background dealing with this issue, I've also had some related personal experiences to share. One evening, while I was driving home in the rain from a holiday party at my parents' house, a car suddenly sped by me, going way too fast given the weather conditions. I heard a calm voice in my head say, "He's going to lose control and hit the car behind him." No emotion or fear came over me. I simply heard a voice that was quiet, calm, and almost peaceful. I glanced up to check which exit I was near, and about five seconds later, the racing car spun out and slammed the vehicle behind it. I dialed 911 on my cell phone within seconds and told them the location of the collision as I continued on my journey. A few minutes later, my emotional response surfaced. I felt freaked out and shaken and I pulled over for a good cry.

Intuition can show up in different ways, but usually it's a quiet voice, feeling, or image that comes into your head at an unexpected time. Typically, there is not a lot of emotion behind it. The initial feeling of an intuitive message is almost always very neutral. Urgent sometimes, but not usually scary or upsetting. It's only when we start *thinking* about it that our fear gets triggered or we work up panic or anxiety thinking about how we will respond.

Intuition can also show up as a slight fluttering of anxiety when some person or situation feels "off," but you can't pinpoint a logical reason why. A situation might seem all right on the surface, with nothing reasonable to support your discomfort, but on some level, you're aware of a problem with it. This causes an unsettled feeling in the mind and body because a contradiction is present. Some people tell me they get a strange pain or knot somewhere in their body, often the stomach, when something is not right.

Discerning between intuition and fear is important. Fear that is triggered repeatedly in response to the same situation often keeps people from doing something they should, like flying to visit Grandma. However, ignoring genuine intuition may result in doing something one shouldn't do, like flying to see Grandma when something feels not quite right about making the trip.

A friend of mine was scheduled on PSA flight 182 from Sacramento to San Diego on September 25, 1978. He hadn't been feeling well all morning and got sicker as he was sitting in his plane seat. After a few minutes of suffering, he decided it wasn't worth it, and he would fly home the next day. He deboarded and drove to a friend's house, where he slept in the spare bedroom. Later that day, he heard the phone ring. It was his sister calling his friend to tell her she was sorry, but John had been on the flight that had crashed that morning, killing all aboard. "What plane crash? He's right here!" his friend exclaimed.

Coincidence? Possibly, or maybe his intuition was giving him messages via his body, which he wisely listened to. He told me later that his stomach always responded that way when something was not right, and he had learned over the years to listen to it. I asked him if he had been feeling scared or anxious before the flight or had had some clue something "bad" might happen. He said, "No, none of that. My stomach just kept getting more and more twisty, and I kept hearing a voice in my head say over and over again, 'Get off the plane. You can fly home tomorrow.' I was arguing with that voice about the cost of buying another ticket and how the flight wasn't that long. But the voice got louder and my nausea got so severe, I decided it wasn't worth it."

I ended up going to school with the son of one of the pilots on that plane. He told me once that his mother—who, interestingly enough, married another pilot after his father was killed—gets scared every time her new husband comes home more than five minutes later than expected from a flight. I sincerely hope she got help with her fear because that's a painful way to live. This kind of fear is not intuition, but the type triggered by the trauma of her past experience. If effectively dealt with, she would be free to enjoy more serenity in her life.

The Gift of Fear

With many clients who contact me for help with relationship issues, fears, phobias, and confidence issues, some type of sexual violation in their past turns out to be the root cause of the presenting problem. Often this trauma results in weight issues, another common concern that brings many women to my office.

Having heard many stories of rape and child molestation over the years, I have observed a few commonalities about the circumstances and women's feelings about it. What I hear over and over again by women is that many feel at least partly at fault for what happened. Even though I and probably everyone else in whom they confide assures them they were in no way responsible, many of the victims say that they understand this on an intellectual level, but the damage remains because the pain attached to this violation sits on a deeper level of emotion.

What often comes up is that the female victim initially had a bad feeling or uncertainty about the person who ended up committing the crime: "He was nice, but something about him just seemed 'off.'" Also, they had often been warned by their friends about the person: "My friend Carrie told me she didn't like Lucas, but she couldn't say why. I wish I had listened to her," or "He just seemed so pushy and insisted I go with him alone. Even though it didn't feel right, I went anyway, and I shouldn't have." Sometimes the scene of the violation is suspicious: "I just had a bad feeling about going to that party. I wish I hadn't gone."

There is an excellent book on the topic that I recommend to my clients who talk to me about sexual violation. *The Gift of Fear; and Other Survival Tactics That Keep Us from Violence* by Gavin De Becker, discusses how many victims, at some point before the attack occurred, had a sense that something wasn't right, but chose to ignore these signs with disastrous results. I see this over and over again in my practice, and I think it's important for women to know that they should not always discount their intuition.

Why do women disregard their inner signals and place themselves in danger? Why do they go to the party? Why do they go off alone with someone who doesn't feel right, or agree to a date with someone they don't really feel comfortable with? Why didn't they start screaming when they were first dragged toward a more secluded area of the party where they ended up being violated? The following are some of the rationales I've heard during client sessions:

"Something felt 'off,' but on paper I couldn't think of a reason why not, so I went."

"I knew him from church, so I thought he would be safe. When my heart kept saying not to go, I just overrode those feelings and reminded myself he was a nice Christian boy, telling myself I was just being silly. I was wrong." This one comes up with shocking frequency, so don't assume that just because you meet someone at church, they are necessarily harmless and "good."

"My friend [this could be parents or another respected person] thought he would be great for me and kept pressuring me to go out with him, so I did, even though I didn't want to."

"He insisted I go on a date with him. I wasn't at all interested, but I didn't want to hurt his feelings, so I went." Men's feelings are not as delicate as you might think, so listen to your instincts and decline invitations if you feel uncomfortable.

"Leaving with him didn't feel right, but the reason he gave me made logical sense."

"I knew something about Uncle Joe felt creepy, but when I screamed that I didn't want him to babysit me, I got slapped. Mom didn't listen to me when I told her he made me uncomfortable by watching me get dressed, and she scolded me to stop making things up." Sadly, it is too often the case that when children protest about questionable behavior from a relative or unwanted attention from a stepparent, they are admonished by the parent, who is not ready to face what is really happening, that they are making things up. This communicates to the child that their feelings are not valid, leaving them feeling conflicted, helpless, and unprotected.

"He was so good-looking and giving me so much attention, I got caught up in the excitement and forgot that I really didn't know this guy at all."

Once victims find themselves in a dangerous situation, and the attack begins, their reaction is often surprising. Instead of kicking and screaming and being loud, they freeze. Often I hear such things as, "I was in shock. I didn't know what was going on. I didn't want to cause a scene, but I was suddenly really afraid. He threatened me." The rationalization about not wanting to "cause a scene" is the most frequent thing I hear, and very unfortunate. If there's a time to cause a scene, it's if you suspect you are, or are about to be, victimized!

I hate to say it but young ladies feeling like it's not OK to cause a scene is largely our own fault. We have to stop teaching our children to "be seen and not heard." We have to stop reading them that "boy who cried wolf" story about a child who cried wolf so much when there was no wolf that when danger did arrive no one believed him. This teaches children, particularly girls, that it's not okay to be wrong about a situation. We need to teach our girls to feel comfortable using their words, screaming and hurting someone they think will hurt them. And mostly we must teach our girls that their bodies are sacred, personal, and that if someone does touch them inappropriately that a major crime (not a misunderstanding) has been committed.

For women who have been victimized, healing from the trauma often involves that person forgiving *themselves* for failing to protect themselves, not listening to warnings, drinking too much, or failing to use more caution. Even if the logical mind knows that beating yourself up is nonproductive, on the feeling level where the attached pain and shame live, there is healing work to be done. If you have been victimized know that if you get help you will be loved, supported through the healing process.

A Few Final Words on Fears

The work of healing is not always easy, but personally, I would rather deal with the cost and hassle of getting help for a fear than to never see Kilauea erupt on the island of Hawaii because I was too afraid to get on a plane. Healing is, in itself, a choice, and one that requires courage and open-mindedness.

What frustrates me the most as a practitioner is that with hypnosis, most of these fears are completely solvable, relatively quickly, or at the very least, able to be lessened to a manageable level. For example, with a fear of air travel at least somewhat addressed, the person might be able to fly with special accommodations, such as sitting in an aisle seat in the emergency row. Seeing people suffer so needlessly is a real shame, especially since they are not the only ones who suffer, but others in their lives suffer as well.

I'm reminded of my own hatred of ants. I really do detest them, and my skin crawls just writing about them. I could easily let that affect my lifestyle here in Southern California, which has a ton of ants! However, I choose to live a full life and won't allow my ant loathing to limit me.

Everyone is afraid of something, and whether it's public speaking, failure, success, dating, being alone, or driving on the freeway, fear can be conquered. In doing so, we become stronger, more self-valuing people. In fact, those who are successful in the world are not the ones who are fearless... very few of these people really are. Rather, it's the people who have had fears, faced them, dealt with them, and often healed from them that are the true winners. Their fears do not run the show.

For instance, are you under the impression that the most important leaders and speakers in the world are among the few on the planet not affected by the world's number-one fear, public speaking? Nope. They, too, become anxious, but they push through, get help when they need it, and do it anyway.

Everyone—and yes, that includes you!—is very important to the world. Every person has something they came to this earth to do, and if you are wasting your energy fretting about things that will likely never happen, you are probably not fulfilling your life's mission.

Please, choose to love yourself enough to do what it takes to get past your fears. Not just for yourself but for the sake of everyone that fear effects, every person who doesn't get the benefit of your company because you are afraid of driving or whatever fear plagues you. Remember that the choice is yours.

Chapter 4
Fun with Past-Lives Regressions

Oh No! I Should Have Taken That Past-Lives Training...

Like a lot of hypnotherapists, my first experience with past-life regression happened by accident. I was working with a woman to address a debilitating fear with which she suffered. In session, I used a technique to "Regress to the Cause," which involves having the client visualize the moment in time when the specific fear began, in order to remove the emotional charge. This particular client was in her twenties. I asked her how old she was while she was under hypnosis, and she replied, "Forty-five."

That obviously wasn't true, so I asked, "What year is it?"

She said, "Eighteen ninety-two."

I began thinking, *Uh-oh, I should've taken that past-life regression class after all!* I asked her more questions and received some pretty interesting details. She claimed she had been killed in a farming accident, in a way that related to the fear with which she had presented. I performed a therapeutic process while she was in the hypnotic state to help her release the fear, and we had one more session after that. Her fear vanished, and I never heard from her again. However, I was so fascinated by the experience that I decided to get training on how to do regression therapy.

Most people aren't aware that past-life regressions are a hotly debated issue in the hypnotherapy community. Some people believe in them wholeheartedly, and others think clients are revisiting deeply embedded dreams or images from movies that stuck in their heads. Some hypnotherapists even think that doing past-life regressions at all delegitimizes our profession as a whole.

There is still much to be learned about how the brain stores information, but it is commonly believed that everything we have seen, done, or experienced is stored in the brain somewhere. That is a lot of information… think about how many movies you may have seen in your lifetime.

Personally, I sit in the middle on this. I do believe in reincarnation, but the scientist in me has to acknowledge that I have no way of knowing if the details a client shares with me are actually from a past life or a stored memory of something they once read, watched, or even just heard when someone told them about a long-passed relative. Having said all that, and in my experience, clients who have gone under hypnosis for a past-life regression are frequently able to do one or more of the following:

- Provide verifiable dates, names, and places
- Give historically accurate information about things they could never have experienced in this lifetime
- Speak in languages they don't know or understand
- End relationships with people who aren't good for them. They are able to extricate themselves from certain destructive relationships once they have further clarity on their present issues that are based in the past.
- Experience miraculous healing from lifelong fears and phobias

I've had a few past-life regressions myself, and my experiences have always been full of information relevant to what was going on at that time in my life. Also, I've lived long enough to know that there are things in this world that are not completely understood, and I am willing to accept that the healing power of a past-life regression, whether real or imagined, may be one of those things. Besides, the process is simply fun, both for the person undergoing the regression as well as the practitioner guiding it.

The following stories tell about some of my more interesting past-life regressions with clients.

I Was Cleopatra… or Maybe Not

As I said, although I do believe in reincarnation, I am not always convinced that when a client undergoes a past-life regression, they are recalling an actual past life. My skepticism is justified in part because I notice an increase in the number of calls involving a particular historical figure, right after the History Channel has run a program about them. I still need to thank Josh Gates and his *Expedition Unknown* television series on the Travel Channel for the two male clients who came in after watching it, convinced they were Genghis Khan in a past life. Neither of them appeared to have been, but it was fun doing a regression with both of them, and I am always happy for the business. Other calls include ones from people thinking they were Cleopatra and Queen Elizabeth, particularly after a movie about one of them is aired. The following story is one of those experiences, one that supports my skepticism about past lives.

As often happens around Halloween, I received a call from someone named Cassie, who was convinced that she was Cleopatra in a past life and wished to do a past-life regression to "confirm" this. I always make it clear that these sessions, though amusing and interesting, don't conclusively prove anything. Basically, I let people know they are for entertainment purposes only.

While under hypnotic regression, I had Cassie go back to the time she was most interested in, and asked her to step into her old body. I then asked where she was, and she replied, "Ancient Egypt." Hmm. It seemed she hadn't completely stepped into that old body, because an ancient Egyptian wouldn't describe their present time as "ancient." I asked her to go deeper, and we tried again. She told me she was "Cleopatra," and I thought, *Great! I bet she'll have a great story… this will be fun!*

I'm something of a history buff, so I asked Cassie some questions related to Cleopatra, to see if she would say something I knew to be factual, such as how Cleopatra's brother died. It is believed that Cleopatra murdered him. Cassie didn't know, however. The name of her father, she said, was Ptolemy, which is correct but far from secret information. When I asked for the names of her sons, one of which was also Ptolemy, she only mentioned Caesarion. Again, the name of this son is also fairly common knowledge. My next question was the name of Caesarion's father, and her answer almost made me burst out laughing (fortunately, I didn't). She said in a firm voice, "Titus Pullo."

Some of you may recognize Titus Pullo as the name of a fictional character in a great show called *Rome*, which was run on HBO from 2005 to 2007. Actually, this show was one of my all-time favorites. Although many elements of the show were based on real historical figures, the character Titus Pullo—played by the gorgeous Ray Stevenson—was fictional. In the show, he was Caesarion's father rather than Julius Caesar, whom history tells us was the actual dad.

At this point, fearing she would start getting into more plot details of that show, I moved on to the next phase of the session.

When doing a past-life regression, I always ask the person from the past life if they have a message for the person coming to see me, something that could help them with a problem in this life. What followed was some very good and relevant advice regarding my client Cassie's current boyfriend, whom she hadn't mentioned earlier. She had just discovered that this boyfriend was cheating on her, and she was struggling with what to do about it.

What she received under hypnosis was a directive to love herself, realize she was a queen, and insist on being treated with the respect befitting her station. "It is your duty as a princess to make sure your children have the best father possible. You owe it to them and to yourself not to associate with such lowly men. You, as a goddess and by birthright, deserve the very best, and you debase and harm yourself by allowing someone so unworthy to be so close to you. No woman should do that, especially not you."

It was, all-in-all, some of the best advice on self-love I had heard from guide. I believe she was either tapping into her higher self, or perhaps even channeling a higher being which guided her in dealing with a difficult situation in a truly empowered way. Either that, or perhaps she had, indeed, been Cleopatra in a past life, but had not tapped in well enough to remember details. Who knows or cares since the results were that my client felt much better after the session.

I had never mentioned to Cassie what I knew about Titus Pullo and the television show, which at that point had been off the air for several years. Although it's likely she didn't remember the details of that program consciously, she had stored them unconsciously. The sensible advice from "Cleopatra" made me confident that the session had been valuable to her. In fact, a week later, she e-mailed me to thank me and to let me know that on the way home, she had picked up some boxes, filled them with her boyfriend's things, and put them outside. She would let him be someone else's problem from then on.

While I don't mean to suggest that all past-life regressions are actually deeply embedded memories, I am certain that some are. Fascinating and enjoyable, they can sometimes even be life-changing, if used to help heal a problem rather than to call up a dead soul for the purpose of fact checking the history books.

The SS Officer Past Life

When I first started offering past-life regressions to the public, one of my first clients was Janice, a Jewish accountant convinced that she had been killed in the Holocaust in a past life. She'd had many dreams over the years about living in Germany and being part of World War II, and she wanted more information.

I had been warned by a teacher that if a client has never tried hypnosis before it can be more difficult for the client than it would for someone who has done hypnotherapy in the past. The hypnotic regression process requires more focus and concentration on the part of the client. Those new to hypnosis don't know what to expect, and may become frustrated or upset if they receive too much or too little information, or if the information doesn't make sense to them as was the case with Janice.

Hearing his warnings in my head, I ignored them and agreed to let Janice come in to do a past-life regression and try to find a lifetime that would likely be very traumatic on her first visit. Initially it went well. She was easily hypnotized. As we proceeded, however, things took a quick turn in the southerly direction. When I had her open the door to her past life during World War II, instead of seeing herself as a Jew, she saw herself as a uniformed Nazi Schutzstaffel (SS) officer! She described the uniform with such detail that I was able to verify her description with the help of Google. Under hypnosis, Janice saw herself pushing Jews into train cars.

Before I could give her the suggestion to step back and watch it like a detective rather than stand in her body, she became so shocked and upset by what she was seeing that she spontaneously brought herself out of hypnosis.

"I'm sorry. I can't do this. It's just too much," she cried. She was understandably upset, and I tried to help her calm down by talking about what she had seen. But she was too deeply troubled by the experience and wanted to leave. It wasn't what she had expected to see. Instead of being the victim, she had been the perpetrator, and that was too much for her to bear.

Admittedly this was one of my first professional regressions and I didn't have enough experience to warn her that when you go back in time, you are not always the good guy in the story.

Can you imagine if you found out or thought you were the victim of an unspeakable crime, but learned that instead, you were actually the opposite? Janice wasn't under hypnosis long enough for me to ask more questions and perhaps uncover something useful for her. I would have asked the regressed self why he had become an SS officer, and why he was doing that job. Did he know where the Jews were going? Was he doing this under duress, as an order, or did he truly have malicious intent? Is it even possible she wasn't an officer at all but rather a spy?

When I think about many of the past-life regressions I have done, I strongly suspect that trauma leads to great learning, which continues from one life to the next. Finding the context for Janice's dreams and the images she saw during our session would have been like finding the key to an important lock. In many areas of life, unlocking the truth may sting at first, but embedded within the information is the possibility for true healing.

A Relationship Healed by a Past-Life Regression

I had known Jaclyn for quite some time before she came in for a past-life regression. She was having difficulty communicating with her father, and things were strained between them to an extent they hadn't been before. Jaclyn wondered if there had been an issue in a past life that might have created estrangement.

I used a regression technique where I had her imagine going down a series of halls that represented different lifetimes, with a guide who knew where everything was, there to assist her in finding the lifetime relevant to the present conflict. When she opened the door, I asked her what year it was. She answered, "1908" in German. I know a little bit of German, so I let her keep going in German for a while.

I asked her name. "Fritz," she responded. You can't get more German than that!

"What city are you in?" I asked.

"Lincoln, Nebraska."

I was asking my questions in English, but she persisted answering in German. After a couple of minutes, she had exhausted my high school German, so I requested she speak in English, please.

I asked her about the man who is her father in her present life, and Jaclyn said he was her older brother. "Fritz" was nineteen years old, and he was working on the farm his brother owned. One day, they were using a piece of farm equipment that I surmised was a combine, based on her description of it. Fritz's brother accidentally pushed him off the platform, and he fell under the machine and was killed. Jaclyn relayed that her brother was distraught and felt responsible for what happened. He never got over it.

We then proceeded with a process in which I had Jaclyn imagine speaking with her brother, letting him know he was forgiven for what had happened, freeing him from guilt, and allowing him to be at peace with the situation. When Jaclyn came out of hypnosis, she said she felt better. Surprisingly, her dad called the next day and out of the blue told her he loved her. That regression helped free up the tension between the two of them and things have not been strained between them since.

The most surprising part is that Jaclyn is of Chinese decent and spoke with a heavy accent; she claimed she didn't know any German. Because she was a friend of mine whom I had known a long time, I didn't doubt that she was telling the truth. While she had spoken to me in German for several minutes, she understood everything she had said. Initially, she hadn't even realized she was speaking in German!

During my work with clients, I have heard many different languages from people who claimed the only language they knew was English. While most of us have probably heard enough of several languages over the years to put together a sentence or two while under hypnosis, I still find it fascinating how often this happens, and the phenomenon tends to support my feeling that people actually are experiencing past lives in session.

Winner of the "Most Bizarre"

Saida came in to see me with a common issue for women. She said, "I have an ex that I cannot seem to get rid of. No matter how hard I try to get him out of my life, I always end up getting back together with him when he calls. I really feel there is a past-life link that keeps us together, and I would like to know what that is." That sounded reasonable to me. I thought a past-life regression would be a good approach for her, so we got started.

During our session, we visited three past lives. The first one took place in the late 1950s. My client had been the driver of a car in an accident. Her present-life ex was in the passenger seat and died in that lifetime. I found it odd that in the 1950s, the man wouldn't be the one driving, so I dug deeper into that. Saida stated she was bringing him home from the hospital, where he had had some kind of surgery in his abdomen, possibly an appendectomy. In the accident, the vehicle skidded on ice and collided with another vehicle. He wasn't wearing a seat belt, was thrown from the car and killed. She felt so guilty that her unresolved guilt made her feel like she owed him something, tying her energy to him.

In the next past life, Saida was part of a noble family and had developed a crush on one of the gardeners in the family's staff. When it was arranged for her to marry someone else and move into his home, she was upset that she couldn't be with the man she loved. It wasn't possible.

The final past life was the most dramatic. Getting the year on this one proved problematic. She kept saying, "They don't tell time the way we do."

I responded, "Ask your guide what year it is."

"The guide says around 200 BC."

Then I asked, "Where?"

"I am not sure, but I think it's Mexico. But they don't call it that."

I had her step more fully into the body of the person whose life she was living so that we could get more information. She said, "There was a battle, and I am the daughter of the losing chieftain. They are keeping me as a prize." She then described a ceremony where a priest of some kind bound her to a man whom they called her husband. The priest made a cut on each of their hands, bound their bleeding hands together with cloth, and told them they were sealed together for all time. Saida would never be able to leave him, even in death.

At this point, I was not sure how to help her unseal this, even if it was not real and her mind had made the whole thing up. If it was a metaphor, we still had to reverse it before her unconscious mind would release the pattern/attachment. While she was still under hypnosis, I asked her how she would like to undo this bond. Saida said she wanted to void the agreement because she never made it, nor had she had any say in the matter.

Then she added, "But I can't because he's a powerful priest." Saida had mentioned earlier that she was Catholic. I asked if a Catholic priest could undo it, and she said "yes."

I decided to double down and said, "How about if you imagine the pope undoing it for you, since he can issue annulments?"

"Yes, that would work," Saida exclaimed.

I had her imagine the pope himself come in and issue an annulment releasing her from this eternal contract, so she was now free to choose if she wanted to stay with her ex or not. When she came out of hypnosis, she said she felt free to decide for the first time in her life. A week later, I received an e-mail from her saying she had broken up with her boyfriend, and she believed it was for good this time.

Regardless of whether her mind created these scenarios, or they were legitimate images from past lives, my client believed they were real. Of greatest significance was the result. Finally, Saida felt free of the compulsion to stay with her ex against her better judgment.

Regressive hypnosis techniques are not so much about proving the existence of a past life as much as about feeling better or being freed from a destructive burden or long-standing habit.

A "Past-Life" Rape

Most of the time, the root cause of peoples' problems can easily be identified in the present, but sometimes, when issues are long term, seemingly intractable, and difficult to resolve, it makes sense to explore the conflict at a deeper level through past-life regression.

Such was the situation with my client Mary, who was well over 150 pounds overweight. Given the enormous amount of weight she wanted to lose, she was also working with a doctor and a nutritionist. Extra support is always a good idea in cases like Mary's.

Mary had come in for several hypnotherapy sessions and had experienced some weight loss, but it didn't feel like we had gotten to the heart of what was causing her emotional eating and self-sabotaging behaviors. She had always wanted to do a past-life regression, so she suggested maybe it was time to give that a try.

I utilize several different approaches and techniques for past-life regressions, and often I am looking for something specific, such as a singular event. I had Mary imagine a train with a conductor who was the historian of her unconscious, a resourceful record-keeper who knew where each and every event was located. I then instructed her to tell the conductor to take us back to the original cause of her weight problem. Under hypnosis, I heard her say, "Okay, I'm there."

"How old are you?" I asked.

"Eighteen," she replied.

"What year is it?"

"Nineteen eighty-five."

Since Mary was in her late forties, this clearly wasn't a past life, so I instructed her to repeat the original request to the train conductor. She said, "The conductor says to tell you this is the right place, and to stop telling her otherwise." I tried not to laugh. Her inner conductor had an attitude I'd never experienced before. I liked it!

Moving onward, I had my client tell me what was happening, and she told a story about going to a party while in college. She met a strange guy who persuaded her to go back to his apartment, where he tied her up and raped her! I was stunned. During the intake process and previous sessions, I had asked her several times if she had ever been sexually violated, and the answer had always been "no." I wondered if this was a repressed memory.

I guided her through a process in which she rescued her younger self before the rape, and saved herself from all that pain. We also did a few other processes to influence decisions she might have made in the aftermath of the trauma to protect herself against future assaults. It turned out that on the day she was driving home after being assaulted, she had asked herself if this would have happened if she hadn't been so thin and attractive. Her unconscious mind then decided to put on weight to protect her from being attractive to future rapists. We did a technique to release her from that decision and came up with a new way she could protect herself that didn't interfere with her health or quality of life. Then I brought her out of hypnosis.

Sexual violation is one of the first questions I ask when seeing a weight-loss client, and I asked her why she hadn't told me about the memory. She replied, "I'm not sure. I think I just forgot about that incident. I never saw the person again, and I wanted to put it behind me. It was very traumatizing."

"Did you ever go to the police?"

"No, because I was underage and drinking, and I figured they would just blame me for being drunk. So, I decided it wasn't worth it."

I asked her if she had ever sought counseling to heal the trauma of this rape, and she said she had gone a few times, but didn't feel like it had helped in any way.

My comment was, "Well, for something that serious, a few times might not be enough." I suggested she see a rape counselor. Although Mary told me later that she decided not to go that route, at least it was on her radar now. Perhaps sometime in the future, she'd hear about some therapeutic weekend seminar for rape victims and decide to attend to get some much-needed healing. Either way, she was able to acknowledge out loud what had happened to her, and she was clear about this incident's role in being one of the primary causes of her weight gain.

After our session, Mary made major improvements in her eating habits and lifestyle, and she lost significant amounts of weight. Sadly, as is often the case, once she felt better, she figured she would save money and stop going to her doctor and coming in for sessions. This decision was a continuation of the self-sabotaging behaviors she engaged in before, the ones that kept her from losing weight and keeping it off. I saw her again a year later because she had regained much of the weight. We started the process over again.

I always suspect sexual violation when someone is very overweight and has not been able to release/lose it, particularly if there is no family history of being overweight and the person is unable to shift their habits despite great effort. Sexual violation is the number-one reason I see people hold onto weight, and any form of it not only affects people's weight, but almost every aspect of their emotional health—from their ability to trust members of the opposite sex and have healthy relationships, to their self-esteem/ self-confidence and sense of trust in general, including their ability to feel safe in the world. The importance of healing these issues goes way beyond dropping a few pounds on the scale. It transforms your entire life for the better.

It's hard to watch someone make major shifts, and then stop once they've finally turned a huge corner in their life. But everyone has their own journey, and change, even positive change, is difficult and takes courage, not to mention persistence. Facing particularly ugly memories, like sexual violation, is hard without help and support. Nonetheless, once you start healing your past, you experience a fundamental transformation in how you view yourself and the world. You and your happiness are so important, and *you* are worth every bit of effort you invest.

Chapter 5
Relationships... Another Word for Stress

"I Don't Think My Husband Loves Me"

Karen had called me to schedule an appointment for issues she was having with lack of confidence. As soon as she sat down in my office and we began with my preliminary questions, she immediately started to cry. This client really needed to talk! It turned out that her lack of confidence stemmed from one very specific thing: she didn't think her husband loved her.

Unfortunately, I hear this often, and the person usually has valid reasons to think or feel this way. Karen, however, was different.

"Why do you think he doesn't love you?" I asked as soon as she had calmed down a bit.

"I don't think he ever did," she sniffed. "I was one of those women who didn't follow *The Rules* [she was referring to a self-help book about how to find "Mr. Right," which among other things advocates that a woman never ask a man for the first date] and asked him out first. In fact, I sort of chased him in college. After college, we got married, but I always wondered if he did just because I was convenient and not because he really loved me."

"You mean you suspect he just picked you because he didn't want to bother looking for someone else?" I asked.

"Yes! Exactly," she replied.

"Who asked whom to marry them?"

"He asked me," Karen related, "but at that point, I had been his girlfriend for over two years and my parents kept asking him when he was going to marry me. I'm not sure he actually wanted to."

It sounded to me like some unpleasant memory from her past was getting triggered somehow, causing her to see her relationship with her husband in the worst way possible. I know men can be pretty lazy sometimes, but to marry someone just because it's the easiest route seems a bit further than just about any man would go. I pressed Karen for more information.

Generally speaking, men are not as complicated as women tend to be. It's much more common among women to take some small piece of information and make a huge case for something bad. I was beginning to suspect that this was what might be going on here, at least in part.

"So other than the fact you feel you chased him," I asked, "do you have any other reason to doubt his love? Does he treat you badly? Is he bad to the kids? Cheating? Something else?" I settled into my chair, ready to listen to Karen's version of the same long, predictable story about cheating or emotional abuse I hear with discouraging frequency.

However, what followed was nowhere near that!

Karen said, "No, he's actually a very good man, and he does nice things for me all the time." She went on to list some of the incredibly generous and loving things he did for her. "He knows I hate filling up the car with gas, and when it gets low, he makes a special trip to go get gas for me. He says he gets nervous about me not having cash with me, so he's always putting money in my wallet. Oh, and back to the car... most of the time I don't even know there's something wrong with it or that it needs tires or something, before he has already taken it into the shop." I listened, feeling baffled. He sounded great so far...

"All of that is very nice," she went on, "but I really don't care about it! What really gets me is that he *never ever* says he loves me. I tell him I love him all the time, but he rarely says it to me. Is there something wrong with me?"

I think, *Yes*! but say, "No, of course not. There is something here we want to look at, though."

The fact that she was so upset about not hearing "I love you" told me there were likely a few things going on here, possibly some issues from her childhood about not feeling loved. One of her issues was fairly easy to address, and getting that resolved would only cost her about $15, so I decided to start with that.

"First, I don't think he married you because you were handy," I began. "Marriage is a big deal, and he had two years to decide if you were a match or not, so let's set that aside for now. On your way home from my office, you need to stop at the bookstore and pick up *The Five Love Languages: The Secret to Love That Lasts* by Gary Chapman."

Then I asked her what kind of cookies he likes. "He doesn't like cookies," she told me, "but he's really into something called 'Rose Milk Bubble Tea' we get at this tea place near us." (I know the place and the drink, it is awesome!)

"Great!" I said. "Pick up one of those on the way home, too. It sounds to me like you guys have a love language problem that is very easy to fix." I explained that from what she'd told me, her husband liked to express his love by *doing* things for her. She, on the other hand, only felt love if he actually *said* those words to her. I added that the reverse might be true from his point of view, and it was very possible he might also be feeling a bit like she didn't love him, because by not truly caring about all the "acts of service" he performed to demonstrate his love, she would say the words but not reciprocate in loving actions.

I guided Karen, while under hypnosis, through a process to affirm that she was loved and lovable. We also did some foundational healing work to address wounds from her past that she had also mentioned in our session. As she left, she promised to do what I suggested.

The next day, I got a very pleasant message from *her husband* on my voicemail. "She is going to book more sessions, and I want to pay for them with my account from now on," he told me (apparently, they kept separate credit accounts to avoid the complication of two people using one checking account). He must have really liked the rose milk tea. Mission accomplished!!

Karen and I had several more therapy sessions, during which we worked on healing incidents from her early life that left her feeling unloved by her family, and building confidence in general. By the time we were finished, she told me that her husband now told her at least once a day that he loved her. She said, "I noticed he seems to say it to me about the same time every day. Once I looked over and noticed he had set a pop-up reminder on his phone reminding him to tell me." Cute... really cute. Karen also said how much the Chapman book had helped to completely turn their relationship around, and how much happier they both felt now. I nodded and thought, *Not bad for just $15!*

I also pondered some of the ideas from the earlier book she had mentioned, *The Rules*. My feeling is that while it's probably better, in general, to let the man ask for the first date, there are likely not many men who wouldn't love it if a woman took the initiative. And let's be honest… with shy, engineer-type men, this may be the only way a date will happen. Personally, I married a software engineer, and I asked him out first. In fact, I probably asked him out on our first *five* or so dates until he realized that if he asked me to go somewhere with him, I would probably say "yes." And I don't doubt that he adores me.

The bottom line always is to love yourself enough that no matter what happens with other people, including romantic interests, you are accepting of yourself and secure knowing your place in the world. The real truth is that everything else is just gravy anyway.

"Help! I Need to Be More Submissive"

My 4:00 p.m. appointment was a healthy-looking, attractive woman in her twenties. Her client form said she was here for help with "relationship issues," certainly nothing unusual for me. I knew right away, though, that this woman's spin on it was unique.

"Well, I am here because my spirit guides keep telling me to embrace my feminine side and be more submissive in my relationship with my husband," she began after I'd brought her into my office. Hmm … I'm not one to argue with spirit guides, but that advice seemed sort of unenlightened to me. I also wondered what spirit guide would equate being "submissive" with being "feminine." Instantly, I thought of something.

"By any chance," I asked her, "did you just read *50 Shades of Grey*?" This is a wildly popular, semi-pornographic book about a woman who gets involved with a man who wants her to be sexually submissive.

"No," she replied. "Should I?"

"Not unless you want to," I explained. "Don't buy it, though. One of your girlfriends is sure to give you a copy soon." Safe bet on my part, since by then just about every woman I knew had a copy they'd already read and couldn't wait to pass on to another female friend.

I questioned her further. "When you say submissive, what do you mean?"

She told me, "My boyfriend *[Okay, wait just a second … a moment before it had been her "husband." I made a note of that]* wants me to be more of a traditional woman who cleans, has dinner ready when he gets home, doesn't ask for things, and wants to have sex when and how he wants." She had mentioned earlier that she had her own business, so I was already sensing this lifestyle might be a problem for her.

"Is that what you want?" I asked, staying carefully neutral.

"Well, yes and no," she told me. "I want our relationship to work. You see, we haven't been married long, and it was a really short courtship. We met online while I was living in another state, and after a short time, he asked me to move to California and live with him."

"When you say 'short time,'" I asked, "how short are you talking?"

"About two months. Now we've been together for three months, since I've been here for a month or so."

I said, "I assume since you met online, you didn't actually spend much time physically together before you moved here. Is that true?"

"Yes, he visited me for about a week. I really didn't know him very well." She paused a moment and looked down toward her feet. "I didn't know about his temper."

"Are you guys actually married yet?" I asked.

"Not on paper. But he wanted us to practice acting like we're married, so that if I meet any men, they'll know I'm taken. He gets mad if I introduce him to people as my boyfriend instead of my husband. And when I go somewhere, he wants to know who I'm with and where we're going. He wants to make sure whoever I'm with knows that he and I are a couple."

Demanding a commitment too quickly, insisting you tell them where you are at all times, and being overly territorial are actually red flags that a relationship is an unhealthy one. Some women mistakenly think of these behaviors as "protective" or jealous-but-forgivable signs of their partner's intense love. Women in these types of relationships may go out of their way to always tell their partner where they are so that the other will feel "reassured." In a healthy relationship, however, each person is an individual and has freedom to come and go as they please.

At this point, I was becoming a bit nervous about this woman's safety, because she had brought up her boyfriend's temper a couple times already. Being new in town, she might not know about services available here that support women in abusive relationships. Also, she hadn't said anything about love, stating only that she wanted to "make it work."

I asked her if she felt physically threatened by her boyfriend, and she said, "No. He isn't physically abusive, but he has a bad temper and gets mad at me a lot when I don't do what he wants." *(Uh-oh... another bad sign.)* She went on, "If I could just learn to be more passive and embrace the feminine role in our relationship, then everything would be fine and we would get along great."

Clearing my throat, I commented, "Let's go back to what you were saying about your spirit guide, because to be honest, that doesn't sound like the advice of a 'higher being,' but more like something your partner might say, or a church. Or maybe it's something you think to yourself to try and keep this situation under control."

She admitted that the advice to be more feminine—meaning subservient—actually came from her boyfriend, but insisted that her spirit guides agreed and were pushing her to submit to his wishes. At this point, I was thinking that if I had spirit guides giving me direction like that, I would fire them and go get some new ones! The problem was, if this woman really believed the spirit guide were the voice of her higher self, it would be tricky to tell her I thought they were full of it...

I decided to tread lightly and try a different approach. "What would happen to you if this relationship didn't work out? Would you go home? Would that be so bad?"

After this question, tears came to her eyes and she cried, "No, and you are probably right about the spirit guides. But I am just so embarrassed! Everyone told me this was a bad idea, that I didn't know him very well. Almost everyone who actually met my boyfriend didn't like him. What will they say if I go back?"

Aha! This was a familiar dilemma, and one, I fear, that keeps a lot of women from seeking help and leaving situations that are very bad for them. Often, women blame religious beliefs for obligating them to stay in a relationship that is abusive. Some churches have a stay-married-or-go-to-hell tenet, but I think people frequently use this as an excuse to not take action. The underlying issue is fear: better to stay in a situation that is horrible but at least familiar than leave and be in a situation more terrifying because it is unknown.

I said, "Is avoiding the possibility of ridicule or criticism from your family worth being in a relationship that might not be good for you?"

"I don't know," she sighed. "I sort of feel like if I can figure out how to get along with *him*, then I can get along with anyone."

I considered this viewpoint, then remarked, "Hmm. I'm sure that's a good approach if you're dealing with a bad boss or an annoying neighbor, but probably not with a potential spouse, someone who might be the father of your children and the person you're planning to spend your life with."

It's not my wish, or my right, to tell anyone they should break up with their partner, but in this case, it seemed like she was already thinking about it and was afraid of her family's reaction. "Trust me," I assured her, "if your family loves you they will be far happier to know you ended a relationship that wasn't working and decided to come home than to hear later that you regretted marrying that person. And besides, if they do say anything to you, remind them that it's none of their business!"

A week after our session, I got an e-mail from her, saying that her boyfriend had actually decided to break up with *her*. But rather than go back home to Texas, she had decided to stay here with some friends. She said, "I really like it here... it's always sunny and there is no snow." I was quite pleased to hear that.

I don't claim to be an expert in the ways of spirit guides, angels, or your higher self, but I am quite certain that if you are considering an off-base course of action, the voice in your head telling you to do that is none of the above, but more likely your ego tripping you up. It's always a good idea to get the perspective of a friend or counselor. Talking to them will provide you a more objective view of what's in your head. When we're engulfed in our issues or unhealthy ideas, we can't count on our own muddled brain to pull us out of it and see the situation more clearly.

If you find yourself in an abusive relationship, know that there are safe places you can go and loving people who can help you... people who will not judge or blame you for what happened. You matter, and your life and safety are more important to the world than you could possibly know. This is especially true if you have children who love and depend on you. Demonstrating courage in leaving a bad situation may be one of the greatest examples you can share with them.

The Pain of Parenting

"Don't get me wrong... I love my kids, but if I had it to do over again, I don't think I would have had any," a new female client said to me one day. She went on to share that she and her husband had had a great relationship before they had kids. "We used to have a lot of fun, we got along great, and our sex life was wonderful. Then we had two kids, and now all we do is fight! We haven't had sex in months."

This is something I hear with surprising frequency, and almost everyone saying it thinks they are the only one who feels that way. They also think they're "bad" for even having thoughts like this, let alone expressing them. On television and among friends, I hear about the joys of parenting, but in sessions with clients, the amount of pain and frustration involved comes through loud and clear. The most frequent complaint I hear is that women feel their husband doesn't "help" enough, which I always find amusing because it presupposes that raising their child is exclusively her job, and his is to "help out."

Another thing my clients also say: "He complains loudly when he has to 'babysit' our daughter/son." This one confuses me, as I wonder why it's called "babysitting" when he is taking care of his own child, as opposed to simply being a parent.

One of the worst situations is when the mother is pressured, against her wishes, to give up a successful career in order to stay home and raise their child. A female client who greatly resented giving up her job said, "We sat down with the numbers and figured out that once we pay for daycare, it would only bring in an extra $400 a month for me to be working, so we decided it would be better for me to quit my job and stay home."

Making matters worse, frequently when a woman leaves the workforce for several years to raise a child, she finds it very difficult to go back. After time passes, she has completely lost her place on the "corporate ladder" and usually has to return to a more entry-level position, rather than the one she left. This can be heartbreaking to someone who truly values her career.

Much of the time, when couples look at the cost of having a child, they assume automatically that it's the woman who will stay at home. They then look to see the effect of subtracting daycare from her paycheck rather than seeing childcare as a household expense to which they both contribute. Don't get me wrong, though. Many women want to stay home and raise a child, but others do not and wind up resenting the fact that childcare costs are considered payable from her earnings and not both parents.

One woman reported that her husband told her they "couldn't afford the luxury of her getting to keep her job." She laughed and commented, "At least he is acknowledging that working outside the home is luxurious when compared to staying home and raising little Johnny."

The result is reflected by the many unhappy, depressed women I see in my practice, who feel underappreciated and lonely. They miss the adult interactions they had with coworkers and colleagues, and resent the fact that while their job was only an eight- to ten-hour day, five or six days per week, parenting is a 24-7 commitment.

On the other hand, I also hear a lot of somewhat bitter men, who feel it's unfair that their wives get to "stay home," when some of them would like the opportunity to do that as well. My suggestions to couples on this issue include talking it out, viewing daycare expense as a shared household obligation, and considering dad stay at home if this makes better economical sense. Becoming more common these days are stay-at-home dads, with wives that are the main breadwinners. Many of these stay-at-home dads take classes at night, so that when they do return to the workforce, they have greater earning potential than before. Stay-at-home moms have this option as well but surprisingly many don't take it.

The advice I give to all women who are choosing to leave a career and stay home is to keep something that is theirs alone, whether this is running a small, home-based business, taking college classes part-time, or becoming involved in charity work or some other type of project that enables them to get away from household duties and interact with other adults.

Many of my clients leave jobs, but do part-time consulting work in the industry they left. One woman, a secretary, decided to start a virtual assistant business, working for clients all over the country who needed help but couldn't afford to hire someone. It was a win-win for everyone, allowing her a flexible schedule and enabling her clients to obtain affordable services.

Another situation I encounter often is mothers who don't take credit for what they do, which is evident from their answers on my intake form. One of the questions asks their occupation, and women who are raising young children often write "N/A" or non-applicable as their answer. In light of the arduous, emotionally draining, and largely unrewarded nature of being a parent to young children, it seems to me women are not giving themselves the respect and credit they deserve.

I applauded one woman who wrote in the occupation section that she was "raising twin two-year-old girls, and that's enough." No kidding! That's more than enough, and I was happy that she recognized this.

Before you take that leap into having kids, talk long and thoroughly with your partner about how the family dynamic will change, especially in the area of working and finances. The person who will be paying the majority of the bills should be decided and agreed upon in advance. Remember, if you don't think being a parent will fit your personality or what you want from life, it is definitely okay to remain childless. It's not selfish to say you don't want to be a parent. I think most people would agree that it's better not to have a child at all than to have one who's not really wanted, which is almost a guarantee that person will later suffer confidence and self-esteem issues.

Eternal Sunshine of the Spotless… Whatever

Eternal Sunshine of the Spotless Mind was a great movie released in 2004 starring Jim Carrey and Kate Winslet. In the movie, after hearing that his ex-girlfriend has had a medical procedure to remove all memories of him and their relationship, Carrey's character decides to do the same, leading to a very interesting story…

The reason I like the plot of this movie so much is that, at least once a month, I get a call for what I jokingly call the "Eternal Sunshine procedure," in which someone wants me to help them forget someone or something—sometimes a particular event, but more often a particular person.

Usually, a person (interestingly, more often a man than a woman) calls because they broke up with their girlfriend/boyfriend, or vice versa, but now they can't get that person out of their head. Frequently, the relationship in question seemed to be a good one, but ended suddenly and badly (e.g., the person discovered their significant other had been cheating on them). Other times, the call is from a man who thought a relationship was going well because his girlfriend seemed to be becoming more independent, was doing more of her own things, and needed him less and less. Rather than seeing that as a sign she might be emotionally backing out of the relationship, the man takes this as a positive sign, but is then stunned when she breaks up with him.

For women, what I hear frequently is that they broke up with someone or had already broken up and were doing well healing from it. Then, a few months after the break-up, they get a call, e-mail, or text suggesting their ex wants to get back together. Sent into a tailspin by this, they once again become confused and upset. All the healing work they did goes right out the window in a tidal wave of emotion and doubt.

Another common situation is that a spouse discovered earlier that he or she was being cheated on, but they decide to work it out rather than break up. Time—in some cases, years—in couples' therapy goes by, and even though things are going well in the relationship, the person cheated on still can't get the thought of what happened out of their head.

Such was the case for a client named Brad who had, years before, experienced a rare yet traumatizing event: he found out that his wife (she was his girlfriend at that time) was cheating on him by coming home early from work and walking in on her having sex with another man.

"I knew we were having problems in our relationship and that her alcoholism was getting out of control, but I didn't have any idea it was that bad!" Brad lamented to me as he told me about the shocking situation. "I gave her an ultimatum. She needed to get help for her alcohol issue if there was ever going to be a chance for us."

Surprisingly, as this is not usually the case, Brad's girlfriend checked herself into an inpatient treatment facility and completely turned her life around. She rediscovered her religious roots and started attending regular Alcoholics Anonymous meetings at her church. Their relationship completely turned around and they eventually got married. By the time I met Brad, they had been married for five years and she had been sober for over ten years.

Now they were at a new milestone as a couple—thinking of starting a family. Brad's old feelings, however, were coming up again about the past cheating incident, and he couldn't seem to get that picture of her having sex with another man out of his head. Even though he told me they had a great relationship now, and that she really was a different person than the one who had cheated on him, he was still having trouble letting go.

Part of the problem for him seemed to be residual anger over what had happened. During a session together, he told me, "When it happened, I was in so much shock that I didn't even have time to get mad. Then she was gone for a month in treatment and I missed her so much. When she came back, she wasn't the same person. It was hard to be angry at the woman who returned to me."

Brad and I worked on helping him reach full forgiveness and releasing what had happened. During hypnotherapy, I reinforced the image of who his wife was now, and used another process to help erase the picture from his mind. He felt significant improvement after our work together, but in the end I recommended his getting some additional marriage counseling to possibly help him through any remaining pain from the event.

Being cheated on is so traumatizing and its one of the most difficult relationship issues I see clients struggle with. But in Brad's case it was made much worse by the fact that initially he didn't try to manage his own feelings and instead buried them to become a land mine for later in life when he got triggered again. Doing as much healing work as possible in the moment is one of the greatest (and hardest) things you can do for yourself but it's necessary in order to be balanced and happy.

Another scenario I encounter a lot in which the person wants the Eternal Sunshine procedure is after someone goes through a onetime incident—for example, a "one-night stand" or a drunken trip to a prostitute—and the person is so filled with shame or remorse that they want the whole thing erased from their brain.

My client Sheila was having trouble getting past a one-night stand her husband had had a couple years before. "He was at a trade show with a bunch of friends, and they got very drunk at a bar," she related. "He met a woman whose name he doesn't even remember, and they had sex in her car. He felt so guilty about it, that he confessed right away when he got home from the trip. I was devastated, of course. Still, we have a great relationship, and according to him, that was the first and last time it would ever happen, so I decided I didn't want to end our marriage over it. I truly don't think he is cheating on me, but I can't seem to get it out of my head that he might under the right circumstances. He feels better now that he has 'cleared his conscience' by telling me, but I'm still terribly upset. In fact, I actually wish he hadn't told me! Can you make it so I forget he did?"

This client made me question whether people should always 'fess up to a one-time affair. I am starting to think that most people, like my client, would be devastated and unable to get past it. On some levels, the one who is betrayed probably doesn't even want to know. It might be more merciful if the cheater cleared their conscience with a counselor or therapist who might help them discover if there is something lacking in the marriage that is making them want to stray, and then vow to never do it again. Buying your peace of mind at the expense of someone else's may be honest, but not honorable. Or, just don't cheat. That would fix things too.

"My Ex Cheated... Now Everyone Else Will Pay"

One thing I really do wish I could erase from clients' memories, because it does so much damage to future relationships, is the memory of being cheated on during a past relationship.

When a female client named Joanie came into my office for her first visit, she was already in tears. Her paperwork indicated she was having relationship troubles due to past cheating. I said to her, "I am so sorry! Is your husband cheating on you?"

"No," Joanie sniffed. "At least, I don't think so. My last boyfriend did, though." She went on to explain that her last serious relationship before marrying her current husband was with a man she had expected to marry but didn't. After two years of what she thought was a good—and at times, great even—relationship, she found out he was cheating on her with her best friend. *(Why is it always the best friend? Seriously!)* They broke up, and she eventually met and married the man she is currently with.

Still tearful, she told me, "He is a great guy and I love him so much! I am very lucky to have him, and he has done nothing to make me doubt his loyalty... but it seems like I can't help getting jealous when he's just conversing with another woman. When he comes home late from work, I worry he's out cheating."

"Do you check his e-mails or phone?" I asked.

"Oh, yeah," Joanie admitted. "Plus his Facebook account and laptop! One day, he got sore at me for asking him about text messages he was getting, and he gave me the password to his phone so I could check them myself. We both thought that would help, but it actually made things worse, because now I'm looking at his phone records and wondering who he's calling. He's in sales, so he has a ton of unfamiliar phone numbers there... I'm always suspicious. This lack of trust is literally ruining our great relationship!"

I have seen this frequently in people who have been cheated on, and though I'm reluctant to say this, unless these people get therapy to look at why they chose a cheater in the first place, they are likely to keep dating cheaters. It seems like their dating radar is somewhat out of whack. It's not unwise for people like this to be a bit more cautious about this issue in their relationships, especially if they haven't done any kind of healing work on the earlier trauma. In the absence of therapy, though, even if a person who's been cheated on doesn't choose a cheater as their next partner, they often find themselves dealing with extreme suspiciousness. Obviously, this is really tough on their partner, who, in a way, is being accused of and punished for a crime they didn't commit. This can cause tremendous damage to what might otherwise be a healthy relationship.

In all cases, working on forgiveness is important, but I believe it's more helpful to decide whether you trust someone or not, and stick with that decision. If someone is going to cheat, they'll do it whether or not you're following them around, monitoring their text messages, or spending hours worrying about it. No amount of investigative activity will create a different outcome if the person is destined to cheat. What I believe with 100 percent certainty is that if cheating is an ongoing issue with someone, the cheater will eventually get caught. And that will most likely be by chance, not by obsessing over the possibility.

Remember this and acknowledge that your partner is innocent until proven guilty. By all means, listen to your intuition and don't ignore the warning signs, but don't always assume smoke means fire. From my own experience, I remember having a nasty fight once with a boyfriend whom I spotted at the mall with one of my girlfriends. When I asked him about it, he said something about running into her at the food court. The way he said this didn't ring true at all, and I sensed it was a lie. I was furious at both of them, only to discover later that they had planned to meet at the mall so she could help him pick out something shiny and sparkly for me for my birthday. It's a good thing I hadn't acted out the physical harm I'd thought about doing to him!

If you have suspicions, take the time to do some research before confronting your partner. Everyone has friends of the opposite sex and not everyone is cheating, although I admit it's more common than you might think.

Unfortunately, it is impossible to *un*-hear something, *un*-see something, and completely forget about an old partner's cheating so you can move on to a new relationship. In many cases, events happening now trigger pain from an earlier similar experience. This is why it's important to do the work involved in healing those old wounds. By working on yourself to let go of the leftover pain from the past, you will certainly grow in self-love. It follows, of course, that the greater value you place on yourself, the less it will matter what others, even the people closest to us, say or do.

"Fix My Wife's Libido, Please"

This particular issue comes up most often as an e-mail sent from the contact form on my website, from men who tell me their wife "never" wants to have sex anymore, and can I "fix" her sex drive? Frequently, it's the husband of a woman who has booked an appointment with me for something else, typically help with losing weight. The husband will write to me to let me know that "she might not say anything about it, but you should know that she needs serious help with her sex drive!" I'm always tempted to laugh… it shows me how very badly many men are craving more sex in their relationships!

I often answer these e-mails by suggesting a few things that would help them get what they want: "Absolutely! I can help her with that if she likes. In the meantime, though, flowers, candy, date nights, and lots of 'I love you's' are always a good idea." Oddly, the men never seem to correspond with me any further after that, but I do get positive feedback from the women who know their husband contacted me.

Libido can be difficult to address, since men and women get turned on by different things, and for both sexes, there may be an underlying physical problem, such as a hormonal imbalance, that is causing or contributing to the issue. However, since I don't deal with hormones in my office, we focus on the emotional side of libido.

If the woman in the relationship is not getting her emotional needs met, it is very hard for her to get excited about sex. Of course, this excludes the women who are married to real jerks, whom they have no interest in having sex with anyway! The most common complaint I hear from women about their partners is that they treat them too much like their mothers. "Honey, what's for dinner? Babe, have you seen my green socks? Where do you want to go for dinner? What do you want to do this weekend? Do I turn left here, or right? Can you do this or that errand? Oh, and by the way, we're out of beer!"

A close second on women's complaints is having way too much to do and not getting enough or often any help from their partner! To be honest, almost every day I hear a woman say, "I work a full day, pick up the kids, come home and make dinner, feed everyone, and clean up… all while he's plopped down in his chair, oblivious to everything that needs to be done. Then he is shocked when, not only do I have zero desire to have sex at the end of the day, but I'm also mad at him and too tired for anything but bed." Not a recipe for a sexy night, that's for sure.

Guys, she wants you to do your share of the household chores, and not just "help out" by taking out the trash after being asked seventeen or so times. If you won't or can't pitch in because of your schedule, propose getting at least a part-time nanny or housekeeper to take some of the load off. Even a stay-at-home mom has a tremendous burden of responsibilities.

Sometimes, your wife or girlfriend wants you to take charge, too. Now I don't mean in a *50 Shades of Grey* kind of way, but perhaps by doing something like planning an entire date without her input. One female client of mine put it best one time when she said, "After a long day of being in charge of the kids, answering questions like 'Can I do this? Where is that? And why can't I have cookies all day?' the last thing I want to hear from my husband on our date night is, 'Where do you want to go?'"

She wants dinner with reservations already made, if required, a movie picked out, preferably with tickets already purchased online, and for heaven's sake, if directions are required get them yourself before you go! Being taken care of, thought about, and treated like a goddess… this is what makes a woman feel sexy.

From the male side of the issue, besides libido problems caused by physical or health-related problems, their chief complaint can pretty much be summarized in one word: sweatpants. Or some equivalent. One male client put it like this: "She wears these awful, stained sweatpants around the house *all the time*. It's like she's just given up on her appearance. Even when we go out on a date, she almost never wears a skirt or something that tells me she wants to look nice for me." Guys seem to be a bit turned on by how others see their woman. If others find her attractive, and he catches men taking an extra glance at her, it makes him proud and very turned on.

The bottom line for better libido starts with everyone having their hormones checked to eliminate that as a problem. Guys, clean the house and pick up dinner on the way home, and don't forget to get her the food she likes. Seal the deal with something shiny in a small box. Ladies, a little something from Victoria's Secret once in a while is basically all they need. Yes, men are a bit easier to please than women, aren't they?

The Prodigal Son Gets the Better Deal

In the famous biblical tale, a man has two sons. One runs off seeking adventure, while the other, more dutiful son remains at home to tend to his father's farm. Years later, the one who left comes back penniless, and the father is so overjoyed at his return, that he announces they will "kill the fatted calf" in celebration. The son who stayed with his father the whole time wonders why there was never a celebration for him. After all, he'd done the "right thing" all along. Why does it appear the other son is the father's favorite?

Admittedly, I never quite got the point of the story, but always felt the more responsible son got the raw end of that deal! Over the years, I've seen similar drama played out in the lives of many of my clients.

My client named Cecelia put it best when she said, "I do everything for my parents, but I am not their favorite. My brother, who doesn't do anything for them, is their favorite!" She went on to tell me that when her parents got sick, she was the one who stepped up to take care of them and make sure they had nursing care when they needed it. She took them "all over town" to doctor's appointments and errands, and yet they rarely thanked her. Instead, she said, she would have to listen to them talk about how great her brother is.

"I spend so much time trying to take care of them, and they don't even really like me. I don't get it," she complained.

"Why do you help them if you feel that way?" I asked her.

Cecelia replied that when her parents really needed help, none of her five siblings were willing to step up. "Some of them say my parents don't need help," she continued. "Others are too busy, or just don't return my phone calls, so I am stuck with the chore."

"Has it occurred to you that the reason your siblings don't step up is because they don't want to, and they know you'll do it if they don't?"

"Yes, but I can't just abandon my parents! They need me."

I asked Cecelia if her parents actually asked for help, and she told me, "No. They just demand, saying things like, 'You need to come at nine to take me to the doctor' without asking if I have plans or if that works for me. I wind up having to drop my plans, and rush off to take them."

After more questions, I learned that Cecelia's parents were actually able to drive, but that they just "didn't like to." Besides, she added, they never asked the doctors the right questions. They had enough money to easily pay for someone to help them, but they didn't want to do that and wanted her to assist them instead.

It doesn't take a genius to see how easy it was for Cecelia's parents to take advantage of her, a family member, and save the expense of hiring someone. It was also a very convenient situation for her siblings, because they didn't want to pitch in and knew their sister would.

"What about just saying 'no' and asking your parents to take care of it themselves or ask a different family member?" This seemed like a pretty straightforward solution!

Cecelia replied, "I would just feel bad for them, and I get guilty if I say 'no.'"

My client's motivation in helping her seemingly overly needy and ungrateful parents needed some examining. I suspected that on some level, she was trying to gain their acceptance. This is a common situation I encounter as a hypnotherapist. At this point, I doubted Cecelia had the clarity to say, "I do it because I want my parents to love me as much as they love my brother," but she might partially admit to this as a reason if questioned directly. Sometimes clients like Cecelia are still trying to win the approval from their parents they never received when they were younger.

The problem with the people-pleasing approach is that it never works. Rare are the cases in which those people they're trying to win over, actually turn around, realize how much that person has done for them, and decide that person is worthy of their love more than someone else. It would be a shocking occurrence if Cecelia's parents said, "You know, Jon was really my baby, but Cecelia is there for us day in, day out. We really love her more, and let's leave her all our money when we die!"

This type of family dynamic is somewhat like dating in high school. Bill is chasing Jennifer, who only sees him as a friend because she is interested in Tom, who doesn't give her the time of day because he is interested in Heather, but that will never go anywhere because Heather is dating a college guy who is only using her for sex. And on it goes… several people not getting what they want because they are not looking at what's right in front of them, the low-hanging fruit. They are only interested in what's running away and uninterested in them. It's the eternal love of the chase.

Over my years in practice, I have seen lots of women come into my office with a similar family dynamic to Cecelia's. Most frequently, these women present initially with issues such as weight loss, depression, or because they want to get along better with their parents. Often, these women have given up opportunities to travel, to marry in some cases, go to school abroad, and basically have a life of their own.

One of these women, Susan, moved in with her dad temporarily after her mother died. She felt her dad needed to be taken care of, and since none of the other siblings would do it, she moved in. Susan stepped into her mother's role and took care of most of the cooking, cleaning, and caring for her dad's three dogs, all the while enduring his mean comments about her weight, long lectures about how she should conduct herself, and other inconsiderate, ungrateful behavior.

After a couple years, one of Susan's siblings asked her why she wasn't paying rent. After all, she was living in their dad's great big house that technically would belong to all of them when he died! It was only fair that she pay rent. Susan was livid, as this same sister had refused to do anything for her father, leaving the burdens to her. Unfortunately, though, like many of my clients in similar situations, rather than stick up for herself and move out, Susan put up with the bullying, agreed to pay a small amount of rent, and stuffed her feelings down with food and an increasingly problematic alcohol problem. In the meantime, her resentment toward her siblings grew greater and deeper.

In the case of another client of mine, Elizabeth, her father was the only source of income for their family of five, but had a stroke when she was a senior in high school. Elizabeth had planned to go away to college, but her mother told her she needed her to stay and help take care of her father and two younger siblings. On a temporary basis, this might have been all right, but as time went on with no improvement in the father's condition, the mother became more and more reliant on Elizabeth and her siblings for money and assistance with their dad. Because Elizabeth had put off her schooling, she was able to get only menial, low-paying jobs.

It became more and more difficult for Elizabeth to leave, and she began to feel extremely guilty any time she left the house to do anything on her own or spent any of the money she earned on herself. Most of Elizabeth's earnings went into a family fund used to help with rent and food for the household.

When I met Elizabeth, she weighed almost three hundred pounds, had dated very little, and was a thirty-five-year-old virgin. She had contacted me for help with losing weight and building confidence to start dating. She was aware living with her parents made her seem a less desirable prospect, and her job environment consisted mostly of women, so she met very few men.

Even though Elizabeth's self-esteem was about as low as a person's can be, when I even suggested she consider moving out and letting her mother take care of her father, she got upset and exclaimed that she couldn't do that! She had to stay home and take care of her dad. I suspected that she somewhat enjoyed the role of caretaker, so I suggested she consider going to school for some kind of healing art, such as nursing. This way, she might build a profession where she filled her need to care for others, and earn a living at the same time.

Elizabeth said that sounded "great," but then kept thinking of reasons why she couldn't do it—no time for class, and who would take care of her mom, dad, and other adult siblings, all of whom were also living at home? The bottom line, I sensed, was that she was scared. There were risks involved with moving out after never being on her own for her whole adult life. Guilt was another factor. She would say, "Who am I to want to live my own life when my parents need me so much?" At our final session together, Elizabeth related how her mother had cried when she suggested she might want to go back to school. "Oh! You can't leave me! What will I do?" In the end, Elizabeth decided to forego working on this issue. I have to assume she is still at home, not living her own life.

This client's mother was actually a skilled manipulator, managing to convince Elizabeth to give up her whole future to stay home and make her own life easier. The sad part is, Elizabeth's mother probably never realized that her treatment and expectations of her daughter and other siblings were basically selfish.

There is, of course, one other significant detail in the dysfunctional family scenario, although clients often won't admit it: the inheritance. Sadly, it is common for me to see people choosing to stay with mom and dad to "help them out" because of their future inheritance, or rather, the fear of being cut out of it. One of the most efficient ways to almost guarantee yourself long-term unhappiness and frustration is to allow a parent to mistreat you for fear of losing an inheritance. Many an overweight woman has told me tale after tale of being treated very badly by an overbearing and bullying parent who doesn't appreciate them, and when I ask why they put up with it, they tell me they are afraid they will lose their inheritance. "My dad owns a big house by the beach. If I make him mad, he'll cut me out of his will… so I put up with it. I call him when he tells me to call, and I let him be mean to me."

The worst part is that it often comes as a nasty surprise when a person spends their whole lives doing as mom and dad wants, and then the parents end up leaving some or all of their money to charity.

I always tell people to just assume there is no inheritance and to live their own lives, but after a lifetime of sacrificing everything for a parent, those habits die hard. While it takes courage to stand up to people and risk angering someone important to you, people overlook that the person who needs to be top priority in their life is *them*! This may sound selfish, but think about it: a truly selfish individual wouldn't have to remind themselves of their own value, or be conflicted about putting their needs first.

The world does not need more martyrs, it needs more courageous people who live up to their fullest potential. Love itself is about the sometimes-delicate balance between giving to others and giving to ourselves. By caring for ourselves first and foremost, we store up enough love inside to share with others in a healthy way—one that doesn't diminish us or those we help.

Mania of a Master Manipulator

I met Amber a while back, when she came to me with what is a sad and surprisingly common situation. She said, "My husband is cheating on me, and he says it's my fault because I've gotten fat." I hate to say it, but I see this same exact issue a couple times per month. It appears lots of men are blaming infidelity on their partner's weight gain; the strange thing is that many times, the client sitting across from me is not very overweight, and often quite attractive.

At the risk of sounding insensitive, I admit I had to stifle a laugh for two reasons when I met Amber. The first was that she was maybe ten pounds over what *Cosmopolitan* magazine would consider her ideal weight, meaning she was around a size 6 rather than a size 4—definitely not what any normal person would consider fat. Second, her husband's talent at manipulation actually had her believing that *his* infidelity was *her* fault, so much so that rather than expressing anger at him in our session, she was totally preoccupied trying to figure out how to lose the weight.

I just had to ask. "By any chance is your husband a professional sales person?"

"No. He's a lawyer." Ah, close enough.

The circumstance here reminded me of something very important I figured out pretty early in life, wisdom I will share with you now from my vast vault of not-always-so-happy life experiences. This is to never underestimate the power of a romantic partner to make you think something *they* did wrong was actually *your* fault.

Now, I am not saying that both partners don't contribute to the problems in a relationship, but seriously… no one makes someone cheat. They choose to do that all on their own, possibly as a response to relationship issues. Obviously, there are healthier ways of handling conflict with a partner. Therapy, for one!

We know that some people are very good at manipulation, and for all I know this man actually believed Amber's weight was the cause of his indiscretion. Most likely, though, he was feeling bad about what he did, and rather than feel guilty (not a pleasant feeling), looked for a way to put the blame on someone else. This is often the case with physical abuse. Plenty of women have said to me, "He said I made him hit me because I made him so mad," or "It's my fault. I could see him getting really angry and I should have walked away, but I didn't."

The bigger question, though, is what would make someone believe such a ridiculous lie? Unfortunately, the answer is life experience and family-of-origin programming. I hate to say it, but usually this faulty information comes from mom. Back in the 1950s, women were taught to take care of a man's needs in a way that this generation is not. The belief was that if a man didn't give a woman what she wanted or needed, there was something wrong with the woman, and she should "try harder" to please him. Even though generations have passed, remnants of that type of socialization still exist.

In a weird way, with cases like Amber's, the woman has to set her emotions aside and go with what is logical. A woman's logical mind would say that if something sounds absurd, it probably is. Unfortunately, the sensitive, insecure part of a person's nature often hears negative comments about their weight or some other characteristic and takes this as truth. Although it is not the truth, it feels like it is. This is where a good girlfriend can be worth her weight in gold.

One time, I remember complaining to a male friend that a man I had been dating stood me up, and then said he did it because I was "too needy." My friend responded, "And when you laughed and told him to get out of your house, how did he respond?"

I didn't say anything to that. My friend said, "What probably happened is that he forgot you guys had plans, but figured that answer would make you mad, so instead he blamed it on you. I can't believe you fell for it. I thought you were more intelligent than that."

Yes, I am more intelligent, but at the time, my date's remark reminded me so much of other painful rejection experiences, a part of me felt it must have been my fault. That part still thought I could avoid the hurt of rejection by changing myself, rather than by just deciding not to date guys who would treat me that way.

The same "blame game" happens for men as well, but I see more women who are victims of this than men. Some people are just highly skilled in the art of manipulation, and their power to hurt and damage others should not be underestimated.

To Amber, I strongly recommended she spend more time with her girlfriends, whom she admitted her husband hated her hanging out with, because he felt after she did she would always come home angry at him. That figured! Those girlfriends were probably wonderful sounding boards, more objective, and in possession of accurate "BS meters."

Amber and I did a small amount of work on weight-loss habits such as curbing stress eating. Really, though, the key for her was to listen more closely to the part of herself that recognized lies. We did quite a bit of processing work on fortifying her sadly slipping confidence. In the end, Amber and her husband attended marriage counseling regarding his infidelity. The last I heard from her, things were going better… not completely resolved, but they had made progress.

Manipulation is an ugly game to play, and if someone says something to you that sounds ridiculous, especially if it makes you cry, run it by a friend. It might just be bulls**t.

Fixable or Not?

"…'til death do us part." In generations past, this period of time wasn't as long as it is today. Not only that, the roles of married men and women used to be much more defined, which kept things—even if limiting—pretty simple. Our "enlightened" era has brought freedom of thought and expanded our possibilities beyond measure, but with that have come magnitudes of complexity.

Professionally speaking, I have yet to hear a client express that they were glad their parents stayed together even though they weren't a good match. Divorce is certainly traumatizing to all parties involved, but so is watching mom and dad fight all the time, as well as living with two unhappy parents. If marriage counseling doesn't work and the only option becomes divorce, children can get through it with help, and they move past this unfortunate reality.

What I do hear in my office, about once a week, in fact, from clients coming in for relationship issues, are things like, "My parents are still together, although my siblings and I have no idea why. These two people clearly hate each other and are both miserable in their relationship. It's hard to watch. If they are staying together for our sake, I wish they would rethink that. We would rather not be the reason they stay unhappy."

I have seen too many people, who are capable of accomplishing truly astonishing things, not following their inner urgings to leave a bad situation and strike out on their own because they feel "making it work" is the right thing to do. Many have expressed feeling trapped in loveless marriages where they didn't feel allowed to do the things they really wanted to do, like go to school, advance their career, or put energy into a business they had started.

My client Darlene, a successful real estate agent, typified this belief. One day, she came into my office crying, and said, "I had a showing scheduled for a 'million-dollar house' [sadly, this is just a 2200-square-foot house in Encinitas, California]. I was so excited about meeting my buyers and just about to leave, when my husband started yelling, 'The kids aren't fed, I want dinner, and you're just running off to play! You can't leave until you do your job!' Well, I *was* leaving to do my job, and if I sold that house, we could more than pay for dinner out that night. But he doesn't care about that. He sees my business pursuits as a selfish luxury I'm only allowed to do when I am done making the house spotless, dealing with the kids, and handling anything else he might need."

As Darlene was telling me all this, I kept thinking of Cinderella and the ball. She went on to say that for the sake of her marriage, she was thinking about leaving her career and focusing on him "at least till the kids are out of the house." Darlene's children were teenagers, and being a real estate agent was probably one of the careers with the most flexible schedule. Although I felt her choice was unfortunate, I knew that ultimately, this was her decision to make.

In this client's case, it sounded to me like her husband might be jealous of her success, and feared losing his hold over her if she made too much of her own money, which could enable her to leave him and find someone less selfish. Also, he sounded like he might be lazy and not want to have to cook or take care of their children.

Either way, he wasn't being very loving or kind toward her and definitely was not supportive of her career.

For people who choose to stay in relationships that aren't working, I think the key is for them to always keep some part of themselves separate. It should be something that nurtures or fulfills them. This could be their own business, owning something special that is all theirs—like a car, perhaps—or a place they go to by themselves, like a spa or retreat where they can feel good, independent of anyone else. One client of mine secretly had a season pass to Disneyland. When his relationship got rough, he would pretend to go to work but instead take a personal day to go there. I thought that was a very healthy thing to do.

Talking is good, but sometimes talking and doing are even better. I had another client named Karen whose husband was actively cheating on her. She had decided not to confront him about it yet and was extremely angry and upset. In this state of mind, it might be hard to have a real conversation with him, but even more difficult to make a rational decision about what she needed to do. She was contemplating many things including divorce, marriage counseling, and inflicting bodily harm on him (she didn't do that one, luckily). I gave her referrals to marriage counselors and a good lawyer, but also gave her some "old school" advice for how to get to a calmer state before she confronted him: I suggested she buy a journal and start writing about how she felt.

Two weeks later, she came in with a medium-sized, one-hundred-page, wire-bound journal, completely full. When I say completely full, I mean she had covered all the pages, both sides, and all the margins. She showed me the journal and all she had written about a million times in the two weeks was one phrase: "F*** you, John!" I found myself having flashbacks of that scene in the movie, *The Shining*, starring Jack Nicholson, where the main character has been supposedly working on a book for weeks, but when his wife looks at his work, she discovers all he has written over and over again is, "All work and no play makes Jack a dull boy."

I was stunned by Karen's efforts, but the best part was that she reported that she felt so much better and was finally able to talk to him calmly about what was going on. They had scheduled an appointment for marriage counseling, and it looked like they were going to get the help they needed.

The key is to insist on getting help. Marriage counseling is not admitting failure in your relationship; it's about setting up better communication between the partners for the sake of the marriage and the kids who have to be around the fighting.

If a person doesn't get help with their relationship issues, even if they decide to leave, they run the risk of creating the same problems in their next relationship. I have seen people who divorced one bad match, only to go on and marry the same type of person, perhaps slightly taller and with a different name! I can't stress enough the importance of getting help for the emotional issues surrounding an unpleasant marriage and divorce, so that you can get the tools to really create the kind of life you most want for yourself and your family.

Having said all that, I am not of the school of thinking that being a martyr and staying in a relationship that is bad for you until you die earns you any special points. I don't mean to knock anyone's religious beliefs, but I personally am not convinced that God or a Higher Power whatever you call it wants us to be miserable, abused, degraded, or sell our soul for the sake of avoiding divorce. Everyone deserves happiness, fulfillment, and a joyful life.

When you are involved in a bad relationship, it can be difficult to conceive getting out of it, but I've seen the other side of this transition—people thriving in a happy marriage to someone who loves and respects them, and children who are also happy living with a stepparent who is a good match for them as well.

You are so very important to the world, and never forget that your happiness matters! Sometimes we have to make decisions and choices for ourselves that people around us, including our partner, family, or children, don't think would be best. However, it is *not* being selfish to put your needs first, especially if it's clear that other people are not. Being first on your own list of priorities gives you the needed foundation to truly offer love to others.

Chapter 6
Fat Shaming Is Not a Weight-Loss Plan

The No-Win of Fat Shaming

Since probably 25 percent of my business is clients coming in for weight loss—although that is not always what we end up working on when they get to my office—this is one of the longer sections of this book and one of the issues I am the most passionate about, so much so that my first book, *Feed Your Real Hunger: Getting off the Emotional Treadmill That Keeps You Overweight*, is entirely about that subject.

Having weighed over 220 pounds myself prior to losing 75 pounds through hypnosis—weight that I have kept off—I understand this issue in a way many so-called weight-loss experts do not. I understand how it feels to be overweight… how frustrating it can be when you feel like you have tried everything, yet can't lose a pound and keep it off for more than ten minutes to save your life. Most importantly, I understand what it's like to be treated as either weak and having no self-control, or even worse, having others act as though you're completely invisible.

Since writing *Feed Your Real Hunger* and working with even more men, women, and teens on this very complex issue, I am strongly convinced that the standard diet and exercise approach put forth in the media has it all wrong. Not only is it wrong, but going that way directs our focus away from the real issues keeping people overweight.

I am deeply troubled by what's commonly called "fat shaming." As the name suggests, this practice attaches a stigma and sense of public shame to overweight people. Some media outlets suggest this is a way of persuading us to eat healthily and lose weight, even going so far as to argue that by not doing this, obesity is being encouraged. I once heard a reporter ask a clothing designer who made plus-sized clothing if making attractive apparel for large women would somehow encourage obesity. The question seemed so utterly ridiculous to me that I totally expected the designer to lash back at the interviewer. Instead, however, she responded that in creating clothing that made women feel good about themselves, they weren't advocating obesity but simply dealing with the reality of the size most women are these days. I liked the answer but it felt like a bit of a cop out.

Making anyone—and it seems more directed toward women than men—feel bad about their weight *does not* make them healthier. Instead, it reinforces low self-esteem and drives overweight people to seek comfort by turning to the very thing that keeps them overweight in the first place, eating too much! Obviously, fat shaming just aggravates the problem, and in my opinion, is a significant factor in why there aren't more female executives, CEO's, and business owners. Certainly, competition with men is another problem women have in reaching their career goals, but it's my strong belief that too many women feel they aren't "good enough" to pursue these positions, have their voices heard, take risks, or command greater respect from those around them.

I cannot tell you how many very well-educated women come into my office feeling that even though they have a PhD in their field, they are a complete failure because they aren't able to do this "one little thing" of controlling their weight. Unfortunately, their feelings of inferiority about this tend to keep them from putting themselves out there more often, speaking up at meetings, or taking on roles of authority.

Remember when Adele won all those Grammy Awards in 2012? There was almost as much media commentary about her weight as there was about her accomplishments. Not only was this very disrespectful to her as a professional, but things like this reinforce to all young girls that no matter what you do in life, your appearance is how you will be judged. This is wrong on multiple levels.

If you consider the issue of obesity, there are millions, possibly billions, of people who have tried the same approach with minimal success. Yet instead of everyone saying, "I did what you told me to do and it didn't work," we point to the person who failed (over and over again, by the way), saying, "No, the approach is sound. You just have no self-control." The error is in blaming all the people who have tried and failed with the same approach for their lack of success, rather than taking a look at the approach and finding out what's missing.

I think the standard guidelines for weight loss fail because they do not address some key emotional and physical factors. In his book *Why We Get Fat*, Gary Taubes suggests that the current approach to dieting being used now is completely wrong, and he has some interesting research to prove it. Another great book, *Salt, Sugar, Fat: How the Food Giants Hooked Us* by Michael Moss, explains how the food industry figured out how to take those three food ingredients and turn them into highly addictive substances.

In my experience with clients, sugar addiction is a major obstacle to people losing weight and keeping it off. That's one aspect of the problem that isn't talked about nearly enough by the mainstream weight-loss community. In the meantime, many of the weight-loss energy bars are so loaded with sugar, they don't look any different from a candy bar to the body.

The emotional part of overeating is also effectively addressed in Sunny Sea Gold's book, *Food: The Good Girl's Drug*. And like any addiction, there are layers of complexity underlying the use of food to handle our feelings. The worst part for people who use food as their drug of choice is that unlike many drug addicts, they can't hide what they are doing because they actually wear their illness on their body. This causes even more shame, which, as mentioned above, only serves to make them feel miserable and vulnerable to using more food to escape the pain. It's a vicious cycle of food, fat, and shame.

In some ways, people using illicit drugs get more respect and sympathy than people whose drug of choice is food. No one says to a cocaine addict that they are just weak. What makes food addiction even worse than other addictions is that a person has to confront their illness constantly, usually at least three times each day, during meals.

A far more complete discussion of the physical and emotional components of weight loss is found in my earlier book. I strongly encourage you to do your own exploration on the issue of weight loss. Be open to new and alternative approaches, and do some research to see how various weight-loss methods and healthy eating programs fcel to you, in order to determine what works. Exploration is the key, and if you stumble on the one to your own weight-loss success, please let me know what it is. I always love to hear what works for people!

The following stories are a sampling of clients' journeys with weight loss—the successes, the failures, and the progress in between.

"Do It for ME!"

I had been working successfully with Carter on building confidence, when he informed me he wanted to work on relationship issues instead. This was not surprising, as these two concerns often go hand-in-hand. In fact, it is the desire to date that usually brings someone in to work on weight-loss issues.

Carter explained, "What I really want is for you to see my best friend and help her lose weight so that I can find her more attractive." Although the desire to date often motivates clients wishing to lose weight, this was a new one on me!

"Carter," I said, "I know you know I can't hypnotize someone remotely without them knowing about it, right? She will actually have to come in."

He laughed. "Yes, I know that, but I think I just wanted to talk to you about it."

"How overweight is she that you don't find her attractive?"

"Well, I don't know her size or how much she weighs," Carter replied, "but I would guess she's well over two hundred pounds. She has a very pretty face, and I do find her somewhat attractive. But … well, I have a problem with the weight."

Having once been young and overweight myself, I had heard plenty of guys say to my brother, "I would totally date your sister if she wasn't so fat." So Carter's words make me cringe, but I respected him for expressing an honest assessment of a physiological response.

I asked Carter, "Do you think she likes you?" It would be silly for him to assume that just because she's overweight, she would welcome any man's attention. Some men seem to believe on some level that they are doing their overweight friend a favor by dating them. This is not the case at all.

"Well, yes. I think so, but I guess I have never asked."

Since men tend to miss the most obvious of signals from women, I assumed any sign of friendliness from her was interpreted by Carter as interest.

"Here's my advice. If you're having difficulty finding her physically attractive now—right now with no changes—she may not be a good match. Quite frankly, unless she is asking you to help her lose weight, which I can guarantee 100 percent she will never do, it's really none of your business. You will just damage your friendship with her if you bring up her weight. I understand that you like her, and she is important to you. As time goes on, the physical attraction may come on its own, but for now, value her just as she is and let her weight be her business. You don't want your love to be conditional before the relationship even gets started. Love her as she is for what she is—a good friend. And if that ever changes, great! If she is truly looking for help, give her my card. I would love to work with her. But if she isn't, be her friend, just like she is yours, and respect her enough to let her decide for herself if she wants help."

I think about how often people lose and gain weight. What if she lost it all, he became very interested in her, and then she put the pounds back on? They might both be heartbroken if that happened, and statistically speaking, it usually does.

I met and dated my husband when I was close to my highest weight. At the time, it didn't work out because I wasn't ready for "the one." We broke up, but remained very good friends. We reconnected romantically later on in life, when I had grown up a bit and had achieved my healthiest weight. My weight wasn't an issue, and I have always felt reassured by the fact that my husband found me attractive when I was at my highest weight. If something should ever happen and I gain it all back, I know he will still love me. I wish that for every woman. But more importantly, what I really wish for all men and women is that they learn to love themselves at any weight they might be.

I will also say that confidence is incredibly sexy. I have a friend who is over 250 pounds. She is a belly dancer and exudes a confidence that is both infectious and magnetic. Whenever we hang out together, men flock to her. Heck, I would date her, and I'm not even gay! This is a woman who would never have to pay for a meal if she didn't want to. It's beautiful to watch, and I greatly admire her, especially when I see super skinny women in my office who won't go to the beach in a bathing suit because they are a size 2 instead of a size 0.

Confidence isn't about losing weight. It's about owning your unique beauty and knowing your worth, regardless of outside circumstances. If you have an overweight friend you wish would lose weight for you, forget it! Leave her or him alone, and learn to love and respect them as they are. Quite frankly, *their* weight is none of *your* business.

As far as things with Carter are concerned, a few months later I saw him again, and this time he brought in a picture of his new, very pretty girlfriend. She was not the one he had wanted me to use my magic wand on. When I asked him about her, though, he told me that during a conversation they'd had, she revealed she was actually a lesbian. In the end, regardless of her weight, he would have struck out anyway. I laughed out loud at this one.

All You Need Is Love... Oh, and to Lose Five Pounds

I sat in my office waiting for my next client, a man asking for my help with confidence and dating issues. Was I ever stunned when the most physically beautiful man I had ever seen came walking in! I thought, *I must have double booked. This guy cannot be having dating problems!*

When he told me he worked as a model and actor, I pretended to be surprised, and then asked him about the issue that had brought him in. He said, "Just like I wrote on my paperwork, I am having trouble finding the right person."

I asked, "Why do you think that is? Because I assume you get hit on all the time."

He went on to explain. "Well, being gay and working in my industry, I do get hit on all the time. The men I meet, though, only seem to be interested in having a fling. Which is okay sometimes, but what I really want is a relationship with marriage, kids, and all that. I think there may be something wrong with me that I can't find what I want."

Twenty minutes earlier, my last client, who was about fifteen pounds overweight, had been complaining about the same thing. With her, she assumed she couldn't find a man because she wasn't pretty enough and needed to lose weight. Now, this man, who looked like a Greek god (and I mean that literally—I'm pretty sure he was Greek), was having the same problem, but assumed it was because of something about him and not his looks. I pondered this one. *If people needed to be prettier than this man to attract true love, there would be no hope for anyone.*

After spending more time with him, I discovered he did have some issues regarding his openness to finding true love. We worked on these during our sessions together. I couldn't help being struck afterward, however, about the bigger picture here. Many people think finding love is about looks, and it's not. If that were true, this man, as well as all the other pretty people in the world, would never be single. Granted, attractive people may have more options than the rest of us, but think about how many celebrity marriages last longer than five years. Almost none! Not only that … attractive celebrity types are not only beautiful, but usually rich as well. Money is the other element most of my male clients seem to think they need to find true love.

Ladies, what the single men in my chair say over and over again is that they want women who are confident, accept and like who they are, and have their own things going on, as opposed to someone who is needy and clingy. They also seem to want women who are healthy and who exercise, because they want someone with an active lifestyle like them. I rarely have a man tell me he wants a super-thin woman who wears a lot of makeup and has breast implants.

Gentlemen, what I hear from women is that they want a man who is willing to invest the time to get to know them, as opposed to expecting sex on the first date. They want a man who likes to do things, has ambition, and is kind. They do not necessarily want a guy who is rich, tall, or especially handsome. Occasionally, women tell me they want a guy who works out, not because of that person's body being more attractive—although yes, that is sometimes part of it—but because they, too, want someone with a healthy, active lifestyle like them.

Universally, men and women tell me they're looking for someone who loves them and treats them with respect. Not surprising. Who doesn't want that?

If you are holding onto the idea that something you are or are not is the reason you can't find love, remember that being happy and comfortable with who you are is far more attractive to both sexes than being thin and rich, but needy and unhappy. Care about yourself enough to work on letting go of these outdated, limiting ideas of what attracts others, and work instead on being confident enough to be open to giving and receiving love.

"Sorry, Lady. You're Too Fat for Heaven"

An elderly client came into my office because, according to her paperwork, she wanted to lose weight. She appeared pretty advanced in years and did not look overweight, so I was surprised and saddened thinking this could be an issue for her. I hoped that perhaps she'd gotten confused filling out the intake form.

Nope.

"So, tell me what I can help you with," I started.

"Well, just like the paperwork says," she replied, "I have some weight to lose."

I jokingly said, "Where? Did your doctor tell you to lose weight? Give me her number. I want to talk to her." She laughed, but then quickly grew silent. Finally, I asked her how much she wanted to lose.

"Oh, no more than ten pounds," she told me.

This seemed a little more logical, but I wanted to know her motivation. I asked her if she was afraid for her health.

She responded, "I have been overweight my entire life, and now that I am eighty years old, I want to finally lick this problem once and for all." That still didn't explain why. I thought, *Oh please, please, please don't let it be something about going to heaven skinny.* As if on cue, she added, "I'm not going to be around much longer, and when I get to heaven, I want to be thin."

A picture formed in my mind of Saint Peter looking at this woman outside the Pearly Gates and saying, "Glad to see you! Great job being a good person your whole life. But first … your weigh-in. We have space considerations up here, too, and fatties take up more room." Fat shaming in Heaven?

I'm no religious expert, and a client's religion is none of my business unless it comes up in a session, but I don't believe Heaven works that way. However, it was her belief system that was relevant, not mine, and so we proceeded.

I asked her how long she had been trying to lose weight.

"Since I was sixteen," she sighed. "So for a long, long time."

"Was it always ten pounds?"

"No, after each of my kids it was a bit more, but never more than twenty pounds. I would always get down to within ten pounds of my goal. It seems like that was the weight my body always went back to." She went on to say she had never been able to shake those ten pounds permanently, and as a result, had never felt comfortable wearing revealing clothing or even a bathing suit in public. This issue had bothered her for most of her life, and she had spent a lot of time, money, and energy trying to resolve it.

I mulled this over. This woman had spent most of her life feeling bad about a mere ten pounds. Many of my clients would kill to be just ten pounds overweight. What most struck me was how she had let these ten pounds affect her mood, level of self-esteem, and probably every eating choice she had ever made throughout her lifetime. It was sad to contemplate the things she might've done if she hadn't given so much attention to this issue. Written an amazing book? Earned a PhD? Invented something? Or even just loved herself wholly and completely (although this is more than most people ever do)?

As a hypnotherapist who works with several people like this woman on body-size issues, I often wonder what society could accomplish as a whole, particularly our young women, if they didn't feel inferior because of their weight. Instead of beating themselves up because they can't control their weight with the typical diet/exercise approach, what if they took a different look at weight loss to find a solution that worked for them? Imagine all the power that could be redirected to positive and productive activities instead of being consumed by obsession and shame!

In the end, I did work with this client on her weight, but I also asked her to consider letting go of the issue at this point in her life so she could focus on being happy with herself and loving the time she had remaining. Sadly, she gave me an answer I've heard many times before: "Oh, I can't do that. That would mean I'll have lived my whole life never accomplishing the one thing I really wanted to do: lose the weight and keep it off." I hope that's not all she really wanted to do, and I hope there is no fat shaming in Heaven.

Extremely Overweight Clients

Over the years, I have had the pleasure of working with many very overweight clients, individuals weighing 260 pounds and over. In nearly all of these cases, one common element I have observed among both men and women is that at some point, they have been a victim of some form of sexual violation, such as rape, incest, molestation, or even being the target of a Peeping Tom.

Female clients usually dress in bulky clothing that not only hides their curves, but is often so oversized it actually makes them appear more overweight than they really are. Also, they frequently wear very little makeup and have androgynous-type hairstyles, detracting further from their appearance, even though many are very pretty. With the men, I observe the results of very little effort given to self-care or grooming. Even if it's blazing hot outside, most come in wearing sweatpants.

I put these severely obese clients in a different category than the ones needing to lose fifty to seventy pounds because the underlying causes of very overweight peoples' condition are usually very different from those of the less afflicted group. The issue with clients having less weight to lose is largely, although not always entirely, habit based. The severely obese individuals generally have a much larger emotional basis underlying their overeating, although habit also plays a role.

James, who was in his thirties and weighed around 280 pounds, contacted me for help in losing weight so he could start dating again. His weight problem began around puberty (very common for both girls and boys), but in spite of trying many different things, he had never been able to shed the pounds and keep them off. James revealed to me that when he was ten years old, a babysitter began molesting him, and this went on for almost two years before he told a parent, who fired the babysitter but never called the police because of the embarrassment this might cause the family. He never got any kind of counseling, nor was the offender ever prosecuted. When it was over, the family simply pretended it never happened, and they didn't talk about it again.

In session, James explained that he had never felt comfortable with his body, as though it didn't belong to him. He also had never gotten help for dealing with his feelings of being violated as a youngster. Instead, he discovered food as a way to handle the feelings he didn't want to face. "I had always been a big eater, but when my parents went through their divorce and attention was in short supply, I would take a box of cereal to my room, and just eat and eat. No one noticed me… it was a great way of hiding." The resulting fat was a great way of hiding, too.

James had always had trouble with meeting women who would go out with him. On the one hand, he felt his weight kept women from finding him attractive. On the other hand, it also protected him from being rejected by them, because he never even got far enough with them that this was a possibility. In a way, James rejected them by hiding behind his weight and keeping women who might otherwise be interested at a distance—literally.

With James, the key to losing weight wasn't about finding the right diet. He'd tried all of them anyway, and they didn't work. The key was to work on healing the younger, smaller self who felt violated, rejected by a family who didn't pay attention to what was going on with him, and who felt that his body was not the sacred gift that it is. He needed to heal his deep wounds if he wanted to let go of the weight and keep it off forever. I explained to James that by addressing these core issues, not only would he lose the weight and keep it off, but he would be able to heal every other area of his life affected by this trauma from his past. Only then would he possibly be able to have a happy, loving relationship with another person.

As I have said before, being overweight is not a problem, but rather the symptom of a problem. If you heal that underlying issue, you can bring healing to all areas of your life, not just the ones you see in the mirror. In the end it's all about love, loving yourself enough to do the deep work of healing so that you can truly be happy and fulfilled. Trust me, *you* are worth the effort.

Weird Causes of Weight Gain

Sexual harassment:

Often when someone has a sudden considerable weight gain I suggest there might be a physical cause. In cases like this, I always suggest the person have a doctor check their hormone levels. If the cause is found not to be physical, it may be emotional. Depending on how significant the emotional basis for the weight gain, this can be quite difficult to fix.

Deidra was in her early twenties and weighed almost three hundred pounds. As if that wasn't serious enough, about fifty pounds of that weight had come on in the previous six months. I asked her what triggered this weight gain, but she responded very vaguely, saying she was eating too many carbs. On her third session, when I could see that we were basically getting nowhere, I said to her, "Look, I feel like something really big is going on here that you aren't sharing. Do you feel comfortable yet telling me what's *really* bothering you in your life right now?"

At that point, Deidra broke down in tears and told me a story that, sadly, I have heard many times with slight variations. She said, "I am being sexually harassed by my boss. He alternates between telling me I look gross because of my weight and trying to get me to come over to his house after work, where I fear he hopes to take advantage of me." Since she worked for a big company with a solid human resources department, I asked her why she didn't tell them what was going on. She said, "I actually worked for this same person before, at a different company, and when I reported him to HR there, I found myself laid off the next week. Granted, it was a big layoff and it could have been coincidence, but I need this job … I can't afford to be out of work right now."

A twist to this particular case was that I happened to know the person who had recently been put in charge of HR at her company, and I knew her to be the kind of person who would never take this issue lightly. I said to Deidra, "I can say with nearly 100 percent certainty that you're likely not the only victim but if you say something you might be the last victim, and you really should report it." Deidra didn't look very reassured by what I said, but I hoped she would take action anyway.

During hypnotherapy, we worked on processes to help her feel safer, cope better with difficult situations, and build her confidence. I also suggested a self-defense class taught by another woman I know, to help her get healthier and feel safe.

The next time I saw Deidra, she told me that she had made friends with one of the HR people who had mentioned in passing (something they are not supposed to do, by the way) that her boss was in trouble because someone had complained about his behavior toward them. She also mentioned that he was being reviewed and was likely going to be fired. Although my client still didn't feel comfortable reporting the issue in spite of my encouragement, she was confident that the problem would be taken care of on its own without her having to do anything.

The reason I encouraged her to complain was not only because it was the right thing to do and could prevent further victimization of both her and others, but also because sticking up for herself would tell both her conscious and unconscious mind that she deserved to be treated with respect and affirm that she would defend and take care of herself when she was being attacked. This is an important message for all of us, because in this way, we are saying to ourselves, "I love you, you deserve the best, and I will defend you no matter the cost." In a world where, sadly, there are few others who will protect you, it is vital for people to trust that they will protect themselves no matter what. No job is ever worth your dignity.

Deidra stopped coming to me before she had achieved her goal weight, but her boss was fired shortly after our last session, and she was well on the way toward regaining her health. I sincerely hope she continued to work on her self-esteem and confidence issues, so that she would truly be able to create the body and life she wanted.

Teen girls and rapid weight gain:

Few things will cause a teen to quickly gain a lot of weight more than sexual violation of any kind, most commonly in the form of being molested in the home by a step-relative, step-parent, step-sibling, or what is most common, the creepy uncle. Since underage sexual molestation is well outside the scope of my practice, whenever someone calls my office and says their teen daughter gained forty pounds in the last six months, I recommend an eating disorder specialist I know who is a psychotherapist as well as a medical doctor. My psychotherapist colleague knows how to ask teen girls about sexual violation in the home, especially when it's a referral from me. This colleague told me I would be surprised how often that is a factor. Actually, she is wrong… I would not be surprised.

New rule! I won't date until…

I had a woman, who had been a widow for about a year, come to me for help with weight loss. She needed to lose probably around fifty pounds. When I asked about her motivation, she said, "I need to start dating again." It was the word "need" that caught my attention, because no one *needs* to date. Most people asking for my help *want* to lose weight so that they feel more desirable to someone else.

I always tell people not to wait until they lose weight to go after the things they want. Start working on getting whatever it is you want now, while you pursue the process of becoming the healthiest version of yourself. Striving for something you want often helps you lose weight.

When I mentioned this to her, she responded with a firm "No! I am *not* going to start dating till I lose fifty pounds." Not wanting to push her too far before she was ready, we got started on some weight-loss and confidence-building techniques, which are always part of my treatment for weight issues.

After a few sessions, this client said that although she was doing (or at least claimed to be doing) all the right things, she wasn't losing much weight. So one day, I again suggested she might rethink her decision to put off dating until after she lost weight. Her reply was the same. "No! Not till I lose fifty pounds!"

At this point, I asked her to ponder if she was really ready to start dating again, since she almost seemed to be sabotaging herself. That's when I got the truth.

Several members of her family had been giving her a hard time about putting her late-husband's death behind her, telling her she should "be over it" by now and needed to move on. Even her late-husband's family kept saying to her that this is what he would want. I tried to put her at ease, joking that since he was dead, he didn't have a say in this. She laughed and agreed.

I suggested that after giving the dating issue some thought, if she decided she wasn't ready, she should allow herself time. "But how long do I give myself?" she asked.

"As long as you need," I told her, "and if that's until the rest of your life, it's all right. There is nothing wrong with being single and having a lot of cats. That's my plan when my husband dies." She laughed again. As a fellow cat lover, she understood what I was telling her.

The great thing was that as soon as she gave herself permission to take as long as she needed before dating, she started to lose weight. It appeared she had been holding onto the weight as a way of keeping herself from having to do something she wasn't ready for yet.

Another client, who worked in public relations in the movie industry, told me she felt being overweight prevented her from getting some clients that she really wanted. One day in session, she let it slip that she was really busy in her business. I then asked her if, on some level, she didn't actually want more clients. She admitted that I could be right. She already had more work than she could really handle, and in a way, being overweight in an industry that puts a high value on thinness was keeping her business from being out-of-control busy. I asked her if there might be another way to manage her business that would allow her to create the body and life she wanted. She finally acknowledged that she could hire an assistant, or even temporary help, to get her over her most hectic time.

When this client finally did get help with her business, she was able to both lose weight and create greater prosperity for herself in a way that made sense and allowed for all her needs to be met.

I told the story in my first book of a woman whose husband wouldn't take her on a promised cruise/belated honeymoon until after she had lost fifty pounds. This would put her at a weight, by the way, that was less than what she had weighed in high school! As an update to that story, I can report that she and her husband are now divorced, and she is much happier.

Over the years, I have seen quite a few people create rules around losing weight, swearing they won't do this or that before they achieve their goal. In my experience, rules like these are usually either a form of self-punishment or a way to avoid something they don't want to face yet. Often, a major thing very obese people are evading is having to deal with the unfamiliarity of their life without all that weight. Would people still love them? Would they suddenly be flooded with unwanted attention from the opposite sex? Would they still find their overweight husband attractive if they lost all the weight? If they didn't, they'd ruin their marriage. Would losing weight mean they could never eat "fun" food again? The truth is, all of these are unknown factors, and you should address them if you decide to embark on a weight-loss journey. In fact, paint a full picture in your mind of what life will really be like when you reach your ideal weight, so that it becomes a more comfortable and less frightening prospect.

Final Thoughts on Weight Loss

To sum up, I don't think most weight-loss advice, particularly the kind that begins and ends with "eat less and exercise more," is addressing the full picture of this complex issue. My experience has shown me that everyone's journey to creating optimal health is a little different. If being overweight is something you struggle with, I encourage you to read as much as you can to educate yourself on the physical and emotional factors contributing to the problem. What I know with 100 percent certainty is that making people feel bad about themselves because of their addiction to food is more a deterrent than a motivation to lose weight. The prevalence of fat shaming is quite literally damaging the self-esteem of our next generation of girls.

Chapter 7
Teens—Smarter Than We Think

Don't Underestimate a Teenager

My hypnotherapy practice has included work with many wonderful young adult men and women. As a general rule, because it's the parents deciding that their child needs help rather than the young adults themselves, the issues tend to be more troublesome to the parent than to the teen. As a result, the challenges I encounter are quite varied, and there's really no teen issue that I see over and over again, as with many of the problems I've discussed up to this point.

The top things I work with teens on are the following:

Weight loss:

This probably represents half of my teenager clientele, but as you will learn in the following section, most of these young adult clients do not actually need help losing weight.

Test-taking anxiety:

I lament that more parents don't get help for their children regarding this issue, because it can be devastating to a young adult's academic career and chances of getting into their first-choice college. Also, it's a fairly simple thing to resolve. I have yet to have to see a teen more than twice for this issue before it goes away, and they are able to comfortably take tests.

Sports performance:

My young clients have included aspiring ballerinas, gymnasts, soccer players, tennis players, volleyball players, and even a couple of junior surfers. The sessions with these athletes have been among my most rewarding and enjoyable because the positive results are seen right away.

Along with the issues above, I have worked with teens on confidence, self-esteem, and dealing with bullies. The results are astounding, making me reflect on how many years of therapy these kids are being spared because the parents brought them in to start confronting these issues when they first became evident, rather than waiting until the effects had fully taken root and created havoc in their young lives.

I would encourage any parent with a troubled teen to try getting them to a good hypnotherapist or psychotherapist. Guiding their coping skills early on will affect the entire course of their lives. It's well worth the cost of a few sessions. Trust me on this one.

Afraid of Vomiting

If someone had told me in hypnotherapy school that one of the most common fears I would be addressing with my clients is fear of vomiting, I would have laughed them off. However, just like with the adults, this is the most common fear I see with teens.

This fear, like that of flying, is more often based in fear of losing control and/or looking bad in front of others. Sometimes it shows up in germaphobes who are more afraid of others vomiting in their presence, although this is less common. Unlike fear of dogs, it usually doesn't have a clear triggering incident. I've seen it start after someone's parents went through a divorce, after the loss of a family pet, and just about everything else. Two things I know for sure: it can be very debilitating, and it's highly treatable with hypnosis.

One day I got a call from the mother of a fourteen-year-old cheerleader named Sarah, who was so afraid of vomiting that her preoccupation with it while competing was distracting her from focusing on her movements, thereby affecting her cheer performance.

As mentioned before, for most people, the basis of this issue is fear of losing control. Sarah had a new spin on it, however. When I asked her if she was afraid of not being able to control her body and vomiting whether she wanted to or not, instead of the usual "Yes, that's it," Sarah said, "No, not really. What actually upsets me is that my friends know I'm afraid of vomiting, and they start making gagging noises to get me upset. Then they make fun of me when I start to cry."

When I see adults in session, I don't allow other people to sit in, because it is too distracting for both me and my client. However, with teens, the parents are allowed to accompany their child during the session. Sarah's mother was there, and when she heard what her daughter said, *she* actually started crying.

"Sarah," she exclaimed, "I had no idea those girls you hang out with were so mean to you! Why didn't you say anything?"

"I tried to, Mom, but you kept saying I needed to stay in cheer and keep busy after school. I like cheer, but the other girls in my class are very mean. That's why I don't go to their sleepovers anymore."

Having heard many similar stories about "mean girls" over the years, I don't know why anyone would ever want to reverse the clock and be a teenager again. Sarah was lacking in confidence, but she was physically very pretty. There are few things as threatening to fellow insecure teens as another pretty girl in a group … and if that pretty girl doesn't have confidence, she makes a great target for being picked on.

Sarah's issues were only partially about being afraid of throwing up. The greater part was being made fun of by her "friends" and looking bad. To most teenagers, ridicule is a traumatic experience. In the end, she and I worked on both the vomiting fear as well as her self-esteem issues, and she was able to get past this and feel better about herself. Several weeks after we had finished therapy, I got an e-mail from her mom saying they had changed cheer schools to one with a coach "less tolerant to bullying." I thought that was an excellent idea.

I would love to say that the problem of being picked on by other girls because you are prettier goes away when you are an adult. Unfortunately, it doesn't. I very frequently have physically beautiful women in my office telling me there is some woman in their office who seems to hate them because they get a lot of male attention. This behavior is rooted in insecurity, and the poignant truth is that many of us never grow out of that insecurity. The more effort you put into loving yourself and knowing who you are as a person separate from your social group, the less it will matter when others make you the target of the negative attitudes they are reflecting about themselves. It's never too late or too early do this work so if you have confidence issues, start now.

Sometimes the Parents Are the Bullies

I love, love, love working with teenagers on weight loss. Having been an overweight teen myself, I know all too well how difficult and emotionally painful it is to be overweight and going through high school. In my first book, *Feed Your Real Hunger: Getting off the Emotional Treadmill That Keeps You Overweight,* I discuss in depth what it's like to be overweight in a world that doesn't always treat large-sized people with the love and respect we all deserve.

While many of the teens I work with come from homes where the parents are loving and supportive partners in their child's efforts to create healthier bodies, at times the parents are putting as much pressure and judgment on their child as the other kids in school!

In fact, in the beach community where I meet my office clients—Encinitas, California—I hear very little about bullying from other kids, and a lot more about the mean, often cruel things the parents say to these teens about their weight, making this problem so much worse for them. I also work with clients in other states over the telephone, and they talk a bit more about bullying from peers, but not as much as you might think.

Very often, the greatest problems regarding a child's struggle with weight are caused by well-intentioned parents trying to spare their children the pain that they themselves experienced in their own life trying to deal with their weight and body image. Unfortunately, they are going about this the wrong way. Sometimes, in parents' attempts to control their children's (usually their daughters') eating, they resort to saying and doing increasingly mean and degrading things to them—things I suspect many of these parents say to themselves about their own weight.

I do think these parents have good intentions at heart or they wouldn't be paying my fees to get their children help, but they are aggravating the problem because they haven't handled their own issues in this area. What is even more surprising is that very often, the worst pressure comes from the parents of teens who really aren't very overweight at all and wouldn't be described as "fat" by most people.

Here are some actual things I have heard clients say when describing their teen daughters:

"She is so bloated and disgusting … it's just gross. I can't see how she can live like that. She is going to get kicked off the cheerleading team for sure." This comment was about a teen who was only slightly bigger than the other cheerleaders. When I asked the teen herself about getting kicked off the cheerleading team, she told me, "No one gets kicked off. We do it for fun."

Another mom said to me, "My daughter is so fat and disgusting, I won't even let her wear shorts in public. She just embarrasses herself when she does it." I asked this parent if her daughter wearing shorts in public embarrassed *her*, and she said, "Of course it does! That's my kid, and how she looks reflects on me."

I responded, "Then *that's* the issue we need to work on with you," pointing out that her slightly overweight daughter's self-esteem was really being damaged by her words. However, the parent declined my suggestion that she and I have some sessions, insisting that her daughter was the only one with a problem.

A different client's parent described her daughter with these words: "Did you ever see those dancing hippos in the *Fantasia* movies? That's what my daughter looks like when she is onstage dancing." This remark was directed at a daughter who was an aspiring ballet dancer. While all these comments by parents shock me, this one stood out in particular, not only because of its cruelty, but because when I met her, she appeared to be almost underweight! I even had her show me her identification, thinking maybe she and her sister had decided to play a joke on me.

I was stunned and a bit nervous about working with her. When I asked her why she had come, she said, "My mom thinks I'm fat. Do you think I'm fat?"

"No. I think you are beautiful," I told her honestly.

She replied, "For a ballet dancer, I might be bigger than ideal if I want to make dance my career, but I'm sixteen and haven't really decided about that. I don't think I'm fat either."

This girl's mother and I had a talk afterward about the mother working on her own personal issues with weight. She admitted that she had really suffered a lot at the hands of her own mother over this issue and agreed she might be part of the problem. I ended up referring them to an eating-disorder specialist, not because I thought the daughter had a disorder … yet. However, I felt the whole family could benefit from learning healthier attitudes about weight.

One of my female adult clients, with whom I was working on confidence issues, told me that one year during her teens, her father had paid her and her three sisters $5 for every pound they lost. I jokingly asked her how many of them developed eating disorders and was staggered by her answer. "All of us. Mine was the worst. I had to be in inpatient treatment for almost six months." Whoa! Obviously, I was not expecting that answer, or I certainly wouldn't have asked the question in such an insensitive way.

By far the worst parent in terms of this issue was a father who pulled me aside after I had had a session with his lovely daughter, and laughingly told me he and his wife had bribed the family doctor to tell their twelve-year-old daughter she had gluten intolerance (potentially a serious medical problem) so that they could try and force her onto the Paleo diet, which is the one they wanted her to follow. I almost wished he hadn't told me because for the past hour I had to listen to this poor girl cry about never being able to have birthday cake again! I explained to the parent that not only was this a cruel lie, but it could become a self-fulfilling prophecy. If she got it into her head that she was allergic to gluten, she might even cause it to be so. Then I made a comment that I probably shouldn't have but I couldn't help myself, "If you keep doing things like that to her you don't need to save up for college, you need to save up for therapy." Surprisingly, I never saw them again. I sincerely hope he really listened to me, but somehow I doubt it.

While I freely admit that we as a society have to do something about the obesity epidemic—and I am not sure what that "something" should be—I say again with 100 percent certainty that fat shaming is not the answer. Instead we should teach your children about eating healthily and respecting their body by feeding it the most nourishing food possible. Teach them to love fresh fruits and vegetables, and about the addictive nature of salt, sugar (especially sugar), and fat. It is my opinion that nutrition education at school is woefully inadequate, so anything you as a parent can do to supplement that education is an improvement.

In an age where teenage girls are developing eating disorders in record numbers, parents should tune into the fact that overweight teens have the same needs and wants as everyone else: love, affection, acceptance, and reinforcement of how amazing they are regardless of how they look. Giving them what they need now, no matter their size or appearance, will teach them to expect to be treated with respect and not to allow anything less than that in their lives, rather than to worry about how they look in "skinny jeans." As a parent, isn't that what you really want for them anyway? If you yourself have self-worth issues related to your weight, seek help. You might just be healing this obstacle for the next generation as well.

"Kid, Stop Messing with My Laptop!"

Occasionally, I get opportunities to work with teens (and adults) who are diagnosed with what was formally known as "Asperger's Syndrome," although it is now called "Autism Spectrum Disorder." These teens are generally extremely gifted with a specific analytical skill set. However, they are at times socially awkward and have a tendency to say inappropriate things. When they say something socially unacceptable or don't pick up on social cues that everyone else does—for example, knowing someone isn't interested when they look away or walk away—they get upset. This often leads to isolation, depression, painful shyness, and fear of interacting with others.

My eleven-year-old Asperger's client, Kenneth, was extremely quiet with everyone except me. He would talk almost nonstop for our entire session. An extremely bright teenager, Kenneth didn't have a lot of friends because of social limitations related to his being on the spectrum. When he said the wrong things around his peers, he was ridiculed and embarrassed sometimes. Unfortunately, this caused him to retreat into himself and not make friends.

Kenneth's mom dropped him off a few minutes early one day, so I wasn't quite ready for him. I left him alone in my office for exactly two minutes, so I could make a cup of tea. When I came back, he was in my chair messing around with my laptop. Because we were working together to help him overcome his shyness, I was surprised he would get on my laptop without permission. But before I could say, "Hey, quit that!" he said, "You have a bad video card. I bet you can't play any games with this one."

"Um, I don't play video games on my laptop," I replied, "and would you please stop?"

"Actually, on second thought I think your video card is fine," he went on. "Something else is wrong. Does your screen get all weird when you use certain programs like Excel or Outlook?"

"Well, yes, but I don't think I want you …"

"Oh, I see the problem. You don't have the right driver installed. I could probably fix it if you like." I did mention this kid was eleven, right?

I admit that at this point, I wanted to scream, "Yes! Yes! Yes! Please, please fix it. That's been bugging me for weeks!" But I remembered that he was my client, and his mom was not paying me to let him fix my laptop. In fact, she was paying me because she wanted me to help him be more like his brother, who, she had informed me, was "popular, into sports, and always confident." This brilliant teen in front of me spent most of his time playing video games and creating instructional YouTube videos for gaming using advanced editing software. Yes, he was awkward relating to others and didn't have a ton of friends, but he was absolutely amazing at what he did do well.

After seeing firsthand how bright and intelligent—not to mention helpful—Kenneth was, it struck me that I could help him convey more confidence than he might feel, and work with him to be more comfortable when he did say the wrong things. But, I could *never* teach him or anyone else to be extremely gifted and talented… he had that on his own. I knew his mother loved him, or she wouldn't have brought him in to get him help. I hoped she understood how important he was without any changes at all.

Later, when his mom showed up to collect him, I suggested she consider enrolling him in a programming class or some other sort of advanced computer training.

"Oh, he would love that, but I am not sure we should encourage him there. He needs to be more social, like his brother," she replied.

But the thing was, Kenneth wasn't *like* his brother, nor did he appear to be like his parents. As a result, they seemed to have a tough time relating to him.

"I still think you should," I persisted. "Who knows? You may have a future Bill Gates on your hands."

A few days after that, I received an e-mail from Kenneth's mother saying that she had gone into a computer store and told the clerk she needed the "most complicated video editing software you could buy." At the time it was a program called "After Effects." The clerk strongly recommended she also get training software to go with it. "Absolutely not, I want my son to figure it out on his own," she had told the clerk. She hoped that would keep him busy for a while, but he surprised her by mastering it quickly.

Kenneth told me he used Google a lot when he got stuck. He now has a very popular YouTube channel with a shocking number of followers. I am not going to lie, I am jealous of that. My husband, a software engineer, later confirmed Kenneth's assessment of my laptop. "You should have let him fix it and find out if he's looking for a job."

"He's only eleven," I responded.

"That's too bad," my husband said, "'cause he's probably more mature and definitely more talented than most of the programmers we've hired lately."

Well-meaning parents often try to mold their children to be the way they think the child should be, which is usually similar to how they are. Perhaps it's easier for parents to relate to their kids that way, but it stifles the unique evolution of each child and keeps children from owning their full potential. In my own case, I would find it hard if I had a child who was outgoing, popular, and gregarious— the exact opposite of me. But a child's nature and talents are not for us to decide. Children show up however they show up, and they have the right to explore who they are and their individual potential. The role of parents is to love them, to try to understand them, and to encourage them as they do this. Of course, if your kid's name is Dexter and he wants to be a serial killer… intervention would be totally appropriate and advised. In the end, all they really need is love.

"My Grandfather Was a German Soldier"

One day my youngest teenaged client came in to continue his work on confidence and self-esteem boosting. Typically with this boy, who was particularly shy, I would ask him about video games to get him to talk, after which I was able to move on to other issues. But on this day, he came in and said right away, "I'm sad."

"I'm sorry. Tell me what's going on."

He proceeded to tell me a story that broke my heart. "Veteran's Day is coming up," he began, "and my class is doing an assignment where we talk about our grandfathers' World War II military service. Everyone else's grandfathers were American or British, but mine was on the wrong side. He was a German soldier. The Germans were the bad guys, and I can't tell anyone about that."

I asked him how he was handling it, and he said he wasn't talking to anyone for the duration of this assignment; unfortunately, this was the exact opposite of our goals in therapy!

"People have asked me, but I just say I don't know or shrug them off. He wasn't a Nazi. He was just drafted into the military like everyone else. He lost a leg in the war and suffered greatly like everyone else and yet, he is seen as a bad guy."

As someone with some pretty unsavory things in my family history as well, I understood his feelings. I grew up in Arkansas, where almost everyone is a descendant of someone who fought in the Confederate army during the "War of Northern Aggression," so the Civil War was taught in the schools I went to with a bit more understanding that there were two sides to that conflict. As a teen, I moved to California, where lessons on the Civil War heavily implied that the Confederates were the "bad guys."

While I know it's hard to defend anything or anyone with a connection to the German army during World War II, no child should ever be made to feel ashamed of his family's military service.

I wished this teen could have felt more comfortable sharing about his grandfather with his class. It would have been a good lesson for them, and an opportunity for them to see that there are two sides to every issue, even if one side is clearly in the wrong. It would also be an opportunity for the teacher to talk about how the German citizens were so caught up in the political propaganda, that most of them had no idea about the war atrocities committed.

I really felt for him and this situation. I offered a sympathetic ear to my young client and encouraged him to be proud of his ancestor's military service, the same way the descendant of any soldier should feel, no matter what side they are on. It's easy to get caught up in bias and see things as black and white, good and bad and forget that at the end of the day these were all just people, not so different from you or me. A little understanding and compassion goes a long way toward healing the wounds created by conflict and allowing the past to be the past.

This Girl Could Be President

A teenager named Alicia came in for an appointment that her mother had booked for her, supposedly to help her daughter with "weight loss." Alicia showed up fifteen minutes late, with an attitude that spoke loud and clear that this appointment was not her idea. When I asked her why she had come in, she snapped, "I am here because my mother thinks I am overweight… but I am not. I'm beautiful!"

I immediately liked this kid because she was right on! Alicia wasn't at all overweight, and I wondered what her mom had been thinking. I said, "I agree. You are beautiful and not overweight. So what would you like to work on?"

When she realized I was on her side, Alicia told me she wanted help dealing with her overbearing mother. "You see, I want to be a vegan … er, well I *am* vegan! I don't feel like it's okay to eat animals, and we don't need them for food," she explained. "My mother is concerned that I am getting too many carbs, though, and thinks this will make me overweight. How I look is a big deal to her, but I think she is off-base. I actually keep track of my carbs and am more of a pescatarian vegan, meaning I eat mostly fruit, vegetables, and some fish, but no beef, pork, fowl, dairy, or eggs. My mom is also afraid I won't get enough iron, I think, but there is plenty of that in spinach."

I hate to admit how often I wind up as the referee in arguments between mothers and daughters over carbs! In this case, it sounded like Alicia's mom was also worried about her not getting enough red meat. Because I am not a nutritionist, I let her know I couldn't really comment on the advantages and disadvantages of her pescatarian vegan diet. However, as someone who grew up vegetarian, I was perfectly healthy as a child, except for being overweight, which may or may not have had to do with eating too many carbs.

I commented, "I think your mom is trying to spare you the pain of being overweight, and I suspect she doesn't realize how much you are doing to keep yourself healthy. Perhaps it would be helpful for you both to visit a nutritionist to discuss it. It couldn't hurt, and perhaps your mom will feel more reassured about your choices." Alicia responded that she thought that might be a good idea.

Because we had more time left, I asked her about her future plans. I got an answer I have never heard in my office before. "I plan on becoming a lawyer, then a senator, and then perhaps running for president." Whoa! Now I *really* liked Alicia! And she stated all this with such calm conviction, I believed her. And I was very impressed by her determination.

At the time I saw her, it was well before the 2016 presidential race, so I remarked, "Are you going to be our first female president?"

She said, "Gosh, I hope not. I hope it doesn't take that long. I'm only sixteen. I would like to be the second or third female president."

I was all smiles at this point. Alicia was the kind of girl I liked to see, although rarely do. She knew what she wanted, and she definitely planned to achieve it. She wasn't saying, "I want to be the wife of a senator" but had set her sights way beyond, to being president herself! In my opinion, our society badly needs more girls like Alicia, who haven't bought into the message parents give their children, especially their daughters, far too often: that one's weight and appearance determine their worth and potential.

This teen encouraged me by demonstrating strength and independent thinking at an age when most girls are especially vulnerable to judgment from people around them. As I thought about her later, I wished more parents could instill that kind of belief in their children, and teach them they can be anything they want to be, regardless of body size. Who knows? Another future presidential contender might be sitting across from us at the dinner table!

A Teen Teaches What Weight Loss Won't Do

Jerry was a sixteen-year-old who had come to me for help with improving his self-esteem, which is a common enough issue, especially among teens. What was unusual in Jerry's case was his insight into how his own efforts to boost his confidence hadn't worked.

Jerry told me, "I recently lost a lot of weight, but it didn't give me what I wanted. You see, I thought that if I lost all the weight, I would gain confidence and self-esteem, but that's not what happened at all. In fact, I probably feel less confident than I did before."

I asked him why he felt less confident. "It's hard to explain," he replied, "but I feel like I'm not *me* anymore. Being a 'big boy' was part of who I was. It was my 'thing,' especially being on the football team. Now that I've lost weight, it's hard to know how I fit in. People treat me differently, and I'm not sure I like it. Some people don't seem to know how to treat me at all, since the fat jokes don't work anymore, so they avoid me. I feel kinda lonely and out of place."

I had never had someone more perfectly describe a very common issue among people who lose weight without the help of a counselor to work on the emotional impact of their changed body size. Jerry was exceptional because he was actually able to see for himself how the change made him feel, and he perfectly described one of the reasons why I think so many people who lose significant amounts of weight end up putting it back on.

To some extent, being overweight becomes part of a person's identity, and when that's gone, there is a need for them to adjust and redefine who they are. This is especially hard for teenagers, because losing weight also changes who they are within their social group. If it's a girl, she is no longer the fat, supportive friend. She might now be seen as competition for boys. If it's a boy, he might no longer be seen as the funny, fat friend, and again, may be seen as competition.

This is just as true for adults as it is for teens. When a person goes through a major change like losing a lot of weight, their whole life changes. While they might think those changes will be welcome and positive, change (even if it's for the better) can be difficult because it requires them to make major adjustments. In the case of weight loss, this adjustment is a fundamental one—how a person views him/herself and their place in the world. Losing weight will not make a person confident. They have to do this work separately, each in their own, unique way.

During our sessions together, Jerry and I worked on improving his confidence, and I also helped him see himself as the healthiest version of his body, not defined by his weight but by the whole person he was. We also worked on updating the inner picture he had of himself so that he would reprogram his unconscious mind to say, "This is what I look like now. Let's keep it that way." The new version of him needed to feel more comfortable and familiar than the old version if he was to have any chance of maintaining his healthy weight.

In addition, I guided Jerry through hypnosis processes to ease his adjustment to the changes in his social situation. As I explained to him, "In your adult life, there will be lots of those changes… every time you get a promotion at work, land a major sales deal, or have a big milestone like getting married and starting a family. It's really good that you are learning now how to deal with that."

Sometimes when people leave my office, I fear they won't do the work outside of the session that it takes to heal long term—never read the books I tell them to read, listen to their reinforcement recording, or even remember more than a few words of what I told them. With this teen, I wasn't worried at all because even at his young age, he was able to see what few adults I work with can—the bigger picture behind the problem. Afterward, I was impressed by Jerry's insight and wondered if a future psychotherapist had just left my office.

So often, people in situations like Jerry's don't understand what is occurring at a deeper level, and they end up unconsciously ruining their success and going back to their old weight. Becoming your "inner thin person" is about so much more than just changing what you have for breakfast. It's about changing *who you are* at the breakfast table.

Chapter 8
Steering Clear of Judgment (Isn't Always Easy)

The Moral Compass

Overall, I am pretty good about not judging clients for the things they do. After all, they are sitting in front of me looking for help. To be honest, as a connoisseur of human folly, I usually find the silly things people do to make their lives miserable at least somewhat amusing, but my prime directives dictate against judgment in favor of love and compassion.

Sounds easy, but sometimes, it feels nearly impossible!

Tom had started coming to me for help with relationship issues. He had recently left his wife and three children for another woman, with whom he'd been having an affair for some time. His new relationship wasn't going as smoothly as he would have liked now that they were past the "honeymoon phase" and his new significant other, Tammy, had to deal with the reality of being with a man who had part-time custody of three young children and was going through a very nasty divorce.

To him, I was the only sympathetic ear he had, because his family had basically disowned him for leaving his wife and children, and Tammy was having her own issues about having to play second fiddle to the needs of three kids with recitals, sporting events, graduations of one kind or another, and random health crises.

I admit, there was so much drama that even I had trouble keeping up. It didn't help that he would refer to his soon-to-be ex as his "wife," and then talk about his "girlfriend" in the same sentence. This always had me doing a double take.

One day he told me about the most recent crisis with his girlfriend Tammy. "I wish I could take back something I told her," he complained. "Now she can't seem to stop thinking about it."

"Oh, and what was that?" I asked.

"When I was married to my wife, before I met Tammy, I wasn't getting much sex at home, so me and my buddies would go out sometimes and pay for sex." When I asked him how often he did this, he replied, "A couple of times a month, but it was no big deal! Every guy does it." Immediately my mind interjected, *No, every guy does not do that!* In fact, in my office—which sometimes feels like a church confessional with all the things people tell me—with the exception of military personnel (especially navy men, it seems) on leave, I rarely hear about people hiring prostitutes.

Tom went on, "Now my girlfriend can't seem to forget this! I keep telling her that every guy does it, and probably her other boyfriends have done it and just never told her. She keeps saying she has never been with a man who paid for sex and she's having trouble wrapping her head around it. She doesn't understand that for me it wasn't a big deal! I never kissed them, there was no affection or love… it was just a transaction, like getting a massage."

Definitely, Tom was not a very good salesperson. Not only was he failing to sell Tammy on the idea that this was "no big deal," but he wasn't coming anywhere close to selling me on it, either (even given that, in a sense, he was *paying* me to be sold on it). I am sure that his girlfriend was hearing exactly what I was—someone with no clue that his actions might not have been a good idea, no remorse, and no assurance that he would never do anything like that again. Actually, from the way he was explaining it to me, it sounded like he would do it again if the opportunity presented itself.

I told Tom that I agreed with him that sex with a prostitute can be like a massage to a man and not a personal act of love. However, I then went on to say that Tammy probably took great exception to the fact that first, he had cheated on his wife; second, that he had paid for sex with a prostitute using household money; and last, that his actions had put his ex's health and that of the family at risk. Also, this isn't Holland, and prostitution isn't legal, so he had risked his family's financial future if he were caught and sent to jail.

When I finished, he said in a small voice, "That's funny, because that's just what she said. Hmm. Sounds a bit more serious coming from you than from her."

At this point, I was wondering why he didn't see it the way I did or the way his girlfriend did. Then it occurred to me his moral compass and mine were set differently. While that doesn't necessarily imply that one attitude is "good" and the other "bad," it did mean Tom and I would view these types of situations differently.

One time, I had a conversation with a lawyer in the office down the hall from me who was complaining about a wealthy client who had come to him asking if he could create a dummy corporation where he could hide his income so he could reduce the amount of child support he had to pay. My lawyer friend had told his client, "Not only is that immoral, but it's probably illegal. Either way, I won't be helping you with it." The client was reportedly stunned that he would turn down money to help him do something that he claimed "every business owner does," and my friend had to explain to him that he was sure he would have no problem finding someone to help him, but he wouldn't be signing his name to something like that.

Where morality and values are concerned, people vary widely, and we make a mistake in assuming that those around us think like we do. Tom didn't see the bigger picture of the actions he took, so he didn't understand why anyone would be upset about it. The lawyer's client didn't see why anyone would turn away business doing something that "everyone is doing," regardless of whether it was right or not.

Good people frequently get blindsided by harmful actions from others because they would never think to do those things and don't comprehend that others would. People call those folks "naïve," but that word implies something negative. Personally, I think of them as enlightened individuals who see the good in others first, and that is not a bad way to be. However, if you fall into this category you would do well to consider that this world is full of people, most very different from you, and it's always wise to protect the things you hold dear from those who would mistake your kindness for weakness and thus try to take advantage of you.

I see variations on this theme over and over again in my office, with people going through a divorce. Women in particular say, "It never occurred to me that this man I loved and trusted would do this to me!" They refer to things their ex has done including hiding money in hidden accounts, hiring prostitutes, opening secret credit cards, and putting the family in severe debt without telling them—

debt, by the way, that they both end up being responsible for later.

One client recounted to me that her husband had told her his company needed to send him to Asia to work for the better part of a year, and he spent nine months pretending he was working in Asia when, in truth, he had been transferred to an office in another city within the same state. He only admitted to this after being caught by one of their children. In the next sentence, after I asked her about the divorce proceedings, she said she was letting him handle most of that with a mediator. "He would never cheat me out of my share. I am the mother of his children… he would never do that to me." My next question was whether she had at least checked their credit, to see if he had opened any accounts without her knowledge. Amazingly, she replied she wasn't worried about that kind of thing with him. "Anyone else, yes… but he is a good man."

I pointed out to this client that although her husband might basically be a good man, he had proven that he was capable of being extraordinarily sneaky. She responded, "That's just what my daughter said! She is mad at me for not 'lawyer-ing up' and protecting myself, but I just don't think I need to."

Sadly, here was another example of someone whose denial prevented her from seeing that someone she had trusted was actually unworthy of that loyalty. I wondered how long this illusion would persist and how much she might lose in money and dignity.

While I am an optimist and believe that most people in this world are basically good, I have become more realistic after listening to loads of clients over the years talk about damaging, deceitful things they have done, with seemingly no sense that these things were wrong. I have squirmed in my seat listening to a man talk about "popping his girlfriend in the face" because she mouthed off to him, followed by more justification: "…Not bad like most guys would do, but enough so she wouldn't do it again." One female client talked about making sure her husband's "ex-wives' children," meaning his children, would get nothing when he died. There was another male client who told me he killed his neighbor's dog because it constantly barked. Although it's a difficult struggle, I listen to these stories without judging, because that's not my job. Moreover, I've learned that right and wrong are not the same in everyone's eyes, and misplaced trust can come back to bite the one who believed. Hard.

Expect the best, see the good, but remember to lock your doors at night, and change your computer account passwords now and then. And remember the famous words "trust but verify." This way, you can be not only an optimist, but a *wise* optimist!

Thou Shalt Not Judge a Smoker

My receptionist called to let me know my eleven o'clock appointment had arrived, and recalling that she was coming in for help to quit smoking, I joked, "She's probably going to want a smoke before she comes in."

The receptionist went quiet and replied, "I seriously hope not." I was a bit puzzled by her comment, but found out the reason for it when I walked into the waiting area. Two women sat waiting, and naturally, I approached the one who wasn't pregnant, assuming she was my smoker.

"Tracy?" I ventured.

"I'm Tracy," came the reply from the pregnant woman on the other side of the room.

I thought to myself, *Oh, no! This woman is at least seven months pregnant!*

Once we got to my office and were comfortable, she gave me her story. She had been trying to quit smoking during her entire pregnancy, but was having a hard time. In tears finally, she moaned, "It's starting to become really embarrassing. My boss and coworkers keep judging me."

No shit, I thought immediately. Oops. I suddenly realized from the look on her face that I hadn't just thought that, but it had actually slipped out of my mouth! This was very un-cool on my part, so I immediately apologized.

On a personal level, I was finding this case difficult. It has been my experience that most smokers with children tend to be fairly mindful of not smoking around them. But with this woman, her child couldn't get away from the smoke! It was difficult for me to get past my belief that she was doing something terrible.

Fortunately, she was able to let my momentary lapse of judgment (and tongue) go, and we ended up having a good and healing session.

She e-mailed a month later to tell me she quit the day of our session and was happily smoke-free for the first time since she was sixteen. Obviously, I was happy for her. Unfortunately, though, two months later, after she'd had her baby, she called back to book more sessions. She had picked up cigarettes again the day after she left the hospital and hadn't stopped smoking since.

Quitting smoking and becoming a nonsmoker are two different things. Becoming a nonsmoker requires more work, which this woman was evidently not willing to do, because she was a no-show for her next session.

This can be a tough issue for many. Know it can be resolved, but it does require a real willingness to stop and a decent amount of work to address the emotional issues that underlie the need to pick up a cigarette. The process of quitting cigarettes is likely more intense than you think, but the reward is a lifetime of being free of one of the most detrimental things you can do to your health. As an added bonus, you will no longer be banished to the smoking section near the dumpster every time you need to light up!

And the Pants-on-Fire Award Goes To...

One of my male clients was having trouble getting along with his wife, claiming she was constantly accusing him of cheating, based upon what he called "flimsy evidence" at best.

I didn't even think to ask him outright if he was cheating on his wife, since I assumed he wouldn't be coming to me if that were true. He stated his wife was either paranoid or delusional, so I asked him to give me some examples of the evidence she was using to support her accusations of infidelity.

I struggled to listen quietly to four examples he gave me of times he did "perfectly innocent" things, but his wife thought otherwise. Owing to my experience with clients and peoples' body language, I could tell pretty quickly that he was lying to me. And his explanations for these extremely suspicious actions were so ridiculously concocted, I found it hard to keep a straight face.

At one point, I said, "So when your wife found a woman's t-shirt in your bed that read 'Hot So Hot,' and you told her it belonged to your twelve-year-old daughter, why do you think she didn't believe you?" (At this point, I had to feign a cough to cover a huge belly laugh about to burst out.)

He replied, "I don't know. That's strange, huh." Yeah, it sure was…

I murmured an appropriate "uh-huh" every once in a while as he kept talking, while thinking to myself, *Should I tell him he needs to work on his lying skills if he is going to cheat?* Here I was, a total stranger whose time he was paying for, and I didn't buy any of his stories. Obviously, his wife, who knew him and had likely heard all his absurd explanations before, wasn't buying it either.

I asked him how his relationship with his wife was going otherwise. He said, "Well, I have this nasty habit of lying when my wife confronts me with something. I am so afraid of her anger that I come up with a lie rather than admitting a truth that might make her mad at me."

Ah! Finally, something honest … and something I could help him with.

"Let's go back to the non-cheating incidents. You mentioned you had stayed the night at a woman's house after going drinking with her, but you didn't consider that cheating. Tell me why."

"Well, my wife and I have a volatile relationship right now. We're, like, on and off a lot. When we're 'off,' I move into my brother's house and date other people. When we're 'on,' I move back in, and everything is fine until the next fight. These incidents tend to happen more when we are 'off,' so it's not really cheating, is it? And I don't really have sex with these women." Then, after a pause, "Well, maybe just a little."

I wondered what he considered "just a little sex," but wisely didn't ask since I was not sure I wanted to hear the answer. I cleared my throat and thought maybe it was time for me to try a different approach.

"Are you 'on' now? And how long do these cycles last?"

"Yes, we are," he answered, "but I keep getting e-mails and texts from a woman I met during our 'off' time. My wife finds them and gets mad. I don't unsubscribe to dating sites because I know we will be 'off' again soon, and I don't want to lose traction." (*Wow*, I think. *This is really not cool, but at least I think he's being honest right now.*) He went on, "Typically, the cycles last a couple of months, and then I'm back on my brother's couch."

At this point, our discussion had been focused only on the problems they were having, and I had not heard him say anything about loving his wife or wanting to keep their family together. I decided on the direct approach again and asked him outright why he wanted to stay with her.

"This is my second marriage," he replied, "and I don't want there to be a third. I don't want three baby mamas, three alimony checks to pay, and three women I have to deal with on custody issues." This was the first I had heard him refer to his kids, and I realized this was someone who probably liked being single—a lot. So much so, I figured, that maybe he shouldn't be married to anyone. When I asked him about this, he said his family had also questioned him about this. Truth was, he concluded, he liked being married, saying he had a wife, and he liked being a player, too.

After working with many women who married men like this, often after they've gotten pregnant, I understand the pain they feel. This was the first time, though, that I had heard the man's side of the situation.

I told him, "This is my suggestion. Decide if you want to stay married to this woman and commit to that decision. If you do, it means quitting all those dating sites and perhaps even changing your phone number. If you don't want to stay married, I would suggest spending some time with the idea of staying single for a long time and playing a bit. It sounds like that's what you enjoy doing anyway, whether you are married or not."

He told me he wanted to stay married, so I guided him through a hypnotherapy process supporting his commitment to that decision and all that went along with it. We also worked on helping him catch himself before he engaged in behavior that would cause him to feel like he needed to lie about it.

I suspected he might have a sex addiction since he also talked about watching a lot of porn so I recommended a marriage counselor I know who works on that issue, but I admit I doubt he called her. It was clear to me he had deeper issues than we could clear up in one session and much work to do if he really wanted to change his behavior. People really have to be committed and ready to do that work, two things I doubted he was *yet*. But I hope I planted a seed at least.

Despite my dislike for this client's behavior, I actually liked him quite a bit. He had a certain charisma and charm, which is probably why he was so good at sales, his chosen career. I didn't like him enough to join his harem, but I have to admit that it was pretty entertaining to hear about and I was very glad he came in!

The Cheater I Didn't Like

I have worked with so many people on such a wide variety of issues, that few people surprise me or trigger a strong reaction anymore … which is why I was surprised by how bothered I was by a client who came in for weight loss, although that problem turned out to be just the tip of the iceberg.

In medicine, "fatigue" is a generic symptom that brings a lot of people in to see the doctor and can be caused by many different things. To me, weight loss and confidence issues are what I call the "fatigue" of psychological problems. Both generate a lot of business for me, and yet there is a wide variety of causes. Therefore, when seeing someone for one of these issues, I never know exactly what to expect.

Brenda came in for weight loss, and as is often the case, once she sat down across from a sympathetic listener, she began talking about what was really bothering her.

Brenda was in her early fifties and had lost her husband, Tom, in the past year. I asked her how she was managing the grieving process, and she said, "That's just it. I'm not grieving. You see, I never really loved my husband. I kind of married him for spite."

She launched into a tale that really put my "no judging" directive to the test! Brenda had met Tom while they were both married to other people. He had young children; she had none. They began an affair while working on a trade show together in another country. While enjoying a week-long fling, they mutually decided to go back to their homes, end their respective marriages, and marry each other. She went home and ended hers quickly, but Tom's situation was more complicated. He had children at home and a wife who didn't want to let go, so it took him several years to extricate himself. Tom's wife had initially demanded they go to counseling, which he agreed to, but continued to secretly spend time with Brenda. For her part, she kept pressuring him to "keep his promise to her" and end his marriage. Tom's wife refused to sign the divorce papers, and what followed was several years of back-and-forth negotiations.

After a couple years of this, Brenda, who had long since started to think maybe she and Tom were not a match after all, was about to give up and break up with him. Then, the soon-to-be ex-wife did something that "made it personal" for Brenda. She called Brenda and explained that she was a mother with young kids who wanted to preserve her family, and she asked Brenda as a woman to break up with her husband and leave her family in peace.

Brenda had taken major offense to this. She was so insulted, she put even more pressure on Tom to leave "that woman and her kids" and also did the most she could to make sure the ex got as little as possible in the divorce.

"Didn't she have young children?" I asked.

"Yes, but she knew eventually they were going to get a divorce, so she should have gotten a job or career," Brenda rallied.

Occasionally I see what some might call "shade" directed toward women who work as homemakers from those who secretly wish they could stay home with the kids but instead, for various reasons, pursued a career. Brenda seemed to want the ex to suffer for having done this and not gotten a job. I felt like Brenda was one of those who looked down on women who left the workforce to raise a family. As someone who sees how much work it is to raise children I found this one hard to watch.

A few years after they were finally able to get married, the unthinkable happened. Tom died of a heart attack. This made Brenda, who already had a good income of her own and no children, a very wealthy woman. Meanwhile, the mother of her ex's children and his children received nothing except a small payment on a tiny life insurance policy.

My client seemed to be gloating that the other woman got so little while she got millions in a much larger policy they had bought later.

At this point, I found it a challenge to keep to myself all the things that bothered me about what she was saying—I sympathized so with the ex-wife! I refrained, of course, because I'm not doing my job if I let my own feelings about a situation get in the way of helping a client. I kept hearing the voice of my teacher: "If you get triggered by your client, it's something you need to work on, and if you are unable to deal with why you are getting triggered, and cannot feel neutral with this person, they cannot be your client."

I wound up having a session with my own hypnotherapist after seeing this client, in order to get more perspective. I was being badly triggered here, and I was starting to really dislike my client and that's not doing my job.

Being left destitute had always been a personal fear of mine. I watched my mother, a homemaker her whole life, never make any income on her own, and I always felt this left her in a precarious position. If my dad died or left her for another woman… sure, she would get half of their property, but that wouldn't last long. To this day, my parents remain happily together, but having been poor several times in my life myself, losing all my income has always frightened me. Thankfully, this fear has motivated me to work hard and create income of my own. However, to hear that someone had gone out of her way to ruin the family of another woman and leave her with nothing was a major crime to me, and I had to confront my own issue around this in order to work with this particular client.

Fortunately, with Brenda, this wasn't an issue for long. Two weeks after she came in, I received an e-mail from her saying she didn't think it was a good match. She said, "Basically, I don't like you." She didn't like *me*? Ha! I don't think I had laughed that hard in a long time.

I was glad she came in because the triggering that happened caused me to take a closer look at my fears and how they hold me back. This helped me heal some of the wounding from my own childhood in the process and for that I am truly grateful.

"I Really Blew It, and Now My Marriage Is in Trouble"

I hear these words pretty often, considering I am not a marriage counselor. The people with troubled marriages never tell me that's what they are coming in to see me for, either. Usually, the reason they give is "anxiety."

But the next words out of this particular client's mouth were a first… "I thought my wife was cheating, so I bugged her car with a listening device." I started to yell, "you did what?!!" but fortunately held myself back and instead said:

"So, was she?" I inquired.

"No, but what I did hear really upset me."

I thought to myself, *if he suspects his wife is cheating, it's likely they're already having problems in the marriage.*

Momentarily distracted by the thought, I said, "I'm sorry, but did you say you planted a listening device in your wife's car?"

"Yes," he replied.

"I have to ask. Where did you get it?"

"Oh, that was the easy part," he replied. "I looked online and then found a local store that sells spy gear. I didn't even hide it. I just stuck it in the glove box since she never looks there. But she found out, and now she is talking about leaving me."

"Okay," I said. "Tell me what happened, and we'll start there."

He explained that his wife had been distant and hadn't wanted to have sex in a while. He didn't feel comfortable talking about his wife's lack of sex drive with her, but suspected she might be cheating on him.

"I didn't have any real evidence. I just assumed," he went on. "Fortunately, I was wrong. However, it wasn't all good. You see, one of our four children has special needs, and my wife is her main caregiver. She does the bulk of the work taking care of our daughter. One time when she was alone in her car, going to the gym while I had the kids, she was yelling about how angry she was about what was going on with our daughter. She said some really awful things about her, things I didn't know she felt, and it really upset me. I confronted her, and now she is upset with me for violating her privacy."

Wow. No wonder she was upset. This was a major violation of her privacy.

"What did she say?" I asked.

"She told me she was having an angry rant as a way of blowing off steam. She didn't mean any of it, but mostly, she was mad I was spying on her."

I understood her perspective about the rant. It wasn't difficult to imagine that as the mother of four, driving somewhere might be the only time she was ever completely alone—a great time to have a healthy rant before blowing off more steam at the gym.

"Otherwise, is your wife a good mother? Does she seem to treat all your children with love?"

"Yes, but I can't get past her angry words."

"Could you consider the possibility that she's not lying? She really was just blowing off steam?"

"No. In our religion," he told me, "it's wrong to even think things like that."

I said, "Well, let's face reality. It is human nature to think bad or mean thoughts about people at times. Blowing off steam in the car is a good, nondestructive way of dealing with those feelings."

I couldn't help but think he was trying to use what he perceived as her "wrong" thinking to excuse what was an arguably worse crime on his part, invading her privacy. In the end, we worked on his feelings of anxiety, jealousy, and feeling more comfortable with communication. I also strongly recommended marriage counseling, because this client's issue with his relationship and his fear he was being cheated on seemed far beyond just "anxiety." More work on his part would be needed to identify and talk about his own attitudes, especially how they related to what his wife had said when she *thought* she was by herself.

I am a firm believer that everyone is entitled to privacy and respecting that is an important part of a healthy relationship. Love yourself and your relationships enough to give everyone in your life their privacy.

Be Switzerland

One day I was in my favorite restaurant, Ki's in Encinitas, California, simultaneously eavesdropping on two conversations at once. One young man was deep in conversation with his father, talking about all the different guys he was dating in his quest to find the perfect match. "John is in the military and he's really cute, but he keeps very strange hours and I am not sure I like that. Tim is really great, but he has so much drama following him, I am not sure I can deal with that, and Robert... well, Robert smokes a lot of pot so I am not sure that I want to have more than just a fling with him..." Meanwhile, at another table, a group of very conservative Christians were discussing current political issues from a biblical standpoint. What delighted me was how these two very different groups of people were sharing this lovely space so harmoniously, sipping coffee and eating cake while enjoying the ocean breeze. It seemed like Ki's was Switzerland for that moment—neutral territory where people with major differences in lifestyle and beliefs could be themselves comfortably.

I thought about my hypnotherapy business as I sat there, and hoped that I had achieved this kind of safe neutrality in my practice. In my office, I strive to set any judgments aside to work harmoniously with people of all religious views, races, social backgrounds, or sexual orientation. During the time I spend with clients, my personal political and religious views are irrelevant, unless my client happens to have something in common with me along those lines and it comes up in the conversation.

As a healer, client sessions aren't about me—they're about the people I'm trying to help. The minute a client learns certain things about me, they start thinking about how I might react to what they're sharing, causing them to censor what they say and weakening their potential for healing. To truly reach and help clients, I and the person must start with the truth, no matter what that looks like.

My job is not to make clients think like I do, but rather to help them use the raw materials they have, as well as the lessons from their experiences, and guide them to build the lives they want for themselves. Sometimes this consists of encouraging them to forgive themselves or others; other times, it's showing them how to overcome obstacles left over from their past. Often it is simply to be the one person in their life who believes in them.

I admit this can be very hard, because my first impulse is to jump in and try to save a client from people and situations that I think are not good for them, even though they don't see a problem. An example might be the boyfriend who sounds like a complete scumbag, but whom the client says they love and hope will propose to them. Admittedly, I occasionally make comments to the effect that their relationship dynamic doesn't sound like it's working well for them, but it is outside my scope to tell anyone to stay with or leave anybody. This is for each person to decide for him or herself (even when I have to bite my lip to keep from screaming, "That boyfriend's gotta go!"). To give advice like this might result in their feeling uncomfortable about coming back, which could result in their losing the one objective, nonjudgmental voice they have in their life.

Think how much better all of us would get along if, rather than trying to make people around us be the same as we are, we simply respected them for who they are and where they're at. Remember a few years back when *Duck Dynasty* actor Phil Robertson publicly made those very homophobic comments? My first reaction was to be bothered by them because I emphatically disagreed and have profound respect for gays and lesbians, who face constant challenges to just be themselves. However, I then found myself wondering why I should expect a southern conservative to have the same values and opinions as a Southern California liberal? Robertson has as much right to be who he is as I have to be me. That doesn't mean I will buy anything from him or even watch his show… it's not my "thing." But it's unfair and unrealistic to expect my attitudes to be his or vice versa. Now if he starts writing laws about where my gay, lesbian, and trans friends can use the bathroom *then* we will have a problem.

It would certainly be easier if people felt the same way about every issue, but we're all evolving and changing our perspectives constantly. If everyone felt the same way about everything, think how freaking boring that would be!

The tension and lack of harmony we create in expecting or insisting others be who we think they "should" be makes me wonder why we do this all the time. It must be one of those "human condition" things. The way we respond to it—turning outward against others, or seeking greater acceptance and peace within ourselves (without being victims, mind you)—makes all the difference.

Chapter 9
Confidence

Everyone Is Really Just Faking It

Three main issues make up the bulk of my clients, and they are all very much connected to each other: confidence, weight loss, and anxiety. When you work on any one of these, you are often working on all three. Losing weight often, although not always, helps with confidence, and working on confidence and self-love is an important key to losing weight. The symptom of anxiety can be both the cause and result of problems in the other areas.

Be careful about jumping to conclusions based on how people appear. Many who seem very confident and self-assured are actually faking it (myself included at times). Others may be confident in one area of their lives, but a total mess in other areas; for example, the business owner who is great at making money, but lousy at dating.

Fear is the driving factor in many peoples' lack of confidence. Everyone has fears, and the ones who appear confident are just better at not letting this keep them from their goals.

These next stories include my experiences with clients who came to see me for confidence and self-esteem issues, and later discovered there were more contributing factors than they thought!

Dude, Write the Book Already!

Rob wanted my help with confidence issues. After getting to know him, I learned he had been the victim of the worst school-age bullying I had ever heard. As a sad result, confidence had always been a serious problem for him.

During one of our sessions, he mentioned he had read a book by "a guy with a PhD who has clearly never been bullied before in his life."

"Why do you say that?" I asked.

Rob replied, "Because he had it all wrong. His approach, which he called 'simple,' might be simple, but not easy and wouldn't work. Someone needs to write a book about what it's really like."

Over the years, I have had complaints similar to Rob's regarding most weight-loss books written by people with great credentials, but who, it is evident, had never been overweight and didn't understand what it's like. Clearly, their authors are better at marketing than at writing, because the content is so similar among them that after reading several myself, I felt like I was reading the same three self-help books over and over again. For me, it is pretty easy to spot so-called experts who never struggled with their weight or emotional eating, because they will make statements like, "It's simple. You just stop eating sugar." *Oh, okay! Wow, I totally didn't know that! My weight problems are all solved now. Thanks!* Simple weight-loss solutions are generally not easy, and to flippantly tell others to "just do this" without giving additional strategies is of no help to anyone.

Rob was talking about a serious issue and came from a place of real experience unlike many so-called experts. I asked him, "Why don't *you* write that book?"

He visibly cringed and said, "Oh, I couldn't. I wouldn't want to put my ugly memories out there." I understood that as well; it's hard to share stories when you feel shame and embarrassment about what happened. Rob was working on confidence issues, so I knew this would be hard for him. Still, I felt it would be helpful for him and the world if he could find the courage to write about his experiences, along with the strategies he had used to cope. He had clearly survived, although like the rest of us, he was a work in progress.

Rob agreed with my thoughts on his writing a book, but wasn't yet ready to put all of his stories out there. I encouraged him to start writing, if for no one besides himself. The first book I wrote came almost exclusively from the personal journals I kept during my weight-loss journey. (If you decide to write a book, I suggest doing it on your laptop, not in your journals. It takes a long time to transcribe all those scribbles to your laptop, assuming you can actually read what you wrote… Ask me how I know this.)

I see so many people in my office with amazing experiences and life stories to tell—stories that would motivate and inspire others to pursue their greatest dreams. So few of their voices are heard, unfortunately. It's these quiet real-life experts suffering in silence who truly have something interesting and authentic to share. However, with the issues that result from their experiences, which are often traumatic, the people I see lack confidence in themselves and/or the courage to be vulnerable to the world. Admittedly, "the world" is not always kind.

Having been through the book-writing process a couple times now, I know it's not easy. I also know, though, that it is therapeutic. Some of my most profound healing came from long rants I wrote that were too personal for me to publish. But the physical act of putting the words on paper (virtual paper) was so cleansing that it made me a healthier person. We never know if what we write, especially when the words come from our core, might prompt another to make a positive change in their life. Someday I hope to see Rob's gut-wrenching stories in print because I know how much healing power lies behind those words, but that's not for me to decide. It's his choice.

Maybe it's even time to ask yourself, "What story do *I* need to tell?"

"Holy Asian Fantasy, Batman!"

One day I got a call from a woman with a heavy Asian-sounding accent. She told me she was a massage therapist, but she had a serious problem. "All these people are calling me thinking I offer sexual services with my massage. I don't, but I am getting so many of these calls, it's really starting to feel creepy! I wonder if I am unconsciously making people think that's what I do. On top of that, I get very few calls from women wanting my services, and they are the clients I'd like the most!"

I know from having a massage therapist as an officemate that this is a fairly common problem with massage therapists, so I wasn't surprised by her complaint.

I reassured her that I could probably help, scheduled an appointment, and then checked out her website. Whoa! Holy Asian fantasy, Batman! I wasn't sure what her website designer had been thinking, but the site was certainly eye-catching. First, her headshot featured tousled hair and lots of makeup accenting what some might describe as "bedroom eyes." The background and layout resembled how I imagined an Asian porn site might look. As I exited the website, even *I* was thinking, *does she provide these services, but is lying to me? Why?*

When she came in, she revealed she had only been in this country a couple of years, and her boyfriend, who is not website designer but a hobbyist, had designed the site. The headshot was actually a cropped boudoir shot they had recycled in an effort to save money. Also, not knowing where to advertise her services, she had chosen to put them on Craigslist. Somehow without knowing it, she had succeeded in doing everything to suggest to customers that she was *not* a legitimate massage therapist!

I didn't even discover her biggest mistake until I tried to respond to a message she'd left me. I called and got her voicemail. See if you can spot the problem:

"Hello," comes her very throaty voice (another idea of her boyfriend, I later learned). "I can't take your call now, but leave me a message and I will call you back within two hours." There was, of course, no mention if this two-hour callback applied nights and weekends, too. I could only imagine the kinds of weird voicemail messages she must get.

I immediately suggested a total makeover of her website and marketing strategies. "And before you leave this office you *must* change that voicemail message!" I told her firmly.

During our session, we did a fun process where the client imagines the customers they most want to attract, then pictures a magnet drawing those customers to him or her. I also helped her get in touch with her own intuition, telling her to ask herself what changes she needed to make in order to create a more successful business. As soon as she came out of hypnosis, she said, "I think I need to change my website."

We scheduled a follow-up session, but this time she came in and said, "My boyfriend won't let me change my website. He says you don't know what you're talking about!" *Great*, I thought to myself. *Now I'm arguing with a boyfriend who isn't even here.*

I don't claim to be a marketing genius but I was her target market and her website didn't convey to me what I wanted to see in a massage therapist so I totally disagreed with the boyfriend.

I told her, "I am sure your boyfriend has your best interests at heart (I wasn't sure actually), and it's clear he can design an eye-catching website, but it sounds like you are saying it's not catching the attention of the kinds of customers you want." I again encouraged her to redesign her website. (In this case, even having no website might be better, because the current one might catch the attention of the vice officers at the police department!)

Finally, I had to give her the guidance I've offered many times before to female business owners, but interestingly have never had to share with male business owners. "At the end of the day," I said, "it's your business, and you have to do what you think is best ... not what I think, your boyfriend thinks, or your family thinks, but you. Part of owning a business is making decisions about how you want to run it, rather than taking all the advice your well-meaning, but not necessarily business-savvy, family members dole out. After all, if any of them had what it took to run a successful business, they probably would already be doing it themselves."

Most women have been at least somewhat socialized, from a very young age, to defer to the judgment of men regarding solutions to problems, rather than do what they themselves think is best. As women, this is socialization we need to overcome if we are to feel comfortable and confident enough in ourselves to make important decisions using our own inner wisdom.

I don't think my client cared for my advice, or perhaps she caved to pressure from her boyfriend, but I never saw her again. I do hope I made her think. It's hard being a business owner, and it takes courage to make your own decisions—ones that might be wrong and even costly. If it's your calling to be an entrepreneur, know that this is what's required as part of the game.

"Make Me an Extrovert, Please"

A female programmer named Lois sat across from me in my office. Women in her male-dominated profession aren't that common, so I was happy to meet her. She was here looking for help with the same thing many male engineer-type clients come in for—confidence and dating problems. Her appearance and manner made it somewhat easy to see why she found it hard to date. She was a healthy size, but dressed in shapeless, masculine-looking clothing, with coffee stains on her shirt, thick glasses, no makeup, and an air of don't-bother-me. These things left me with the impression not too many men did.

If she hadn't specified her difficulty was in dating men, I might have thought she was a lesbian. In either case, her style of dress and the air of "don't bother me" she put out wouldn't entirely prevent her from dating, but might make it seem as though she wasn't interested in being approached. Say you go to the grocery store wearing your pajamas, flip-flops, and "hat hair." Looking like this, you seem less open to someone asking for your number than if you are wearing a skirt and makeup.

Lois was not unattractive, just unapproachable. When I questioned her further, she said she was a forty-year-old virgin. She was considering hiring a sexual surrogate because she was embarrassed about being a virgin, and she asked if I knew where she could find one. I am not sure that's even available anymore, and I was afraid to "Google" it for fear my screen would fill up with porn. Needless to say, I didn't know where she could go for that, nor do I think there is anything wrong with being a virgin at any age. But she was embarrassed by it, and it certainly didn't help her feel confident and comfortable with herself so that others would find her approachable.

As a side note, I see a surprising number of forty-year-old virgins of both sexes. In the case of the women, never having sex often seems connected with their being more successful in their career than their male counterparts; for example, being a female officer in the military. With men, I often hear a story about their first girlfriend breaking their heart and their never quite getting over it.

Lois had never dated much earlier in life. I asked her if she had ever considered meeting with an image consultant to assist her in updating her look so she might appear more interested in dating than her clothing and manner would suggest. She became defensive and said she hated that women had to do all that. "It's just wrong that women have to degrade themselves like that," was her comment. I agree that society does seem to expect more from women than it does from men in terms of appearance. In her case, she didn't want to go along with that attitude, so she shouldn't. But maybe there was some other adjustment she would feel comfortable with that might make her appear more approachable. Her defensiveness told me this was an issue for her, so I pressed her a bit more—gently—to see if there was a block we needed to look at.

She told me her mother had pressured her to dress like a "lady" as a young girl and forced her to wear dresses when she didn't want to. Her mother had also been very upset at her choice of professions, telling Lois no man would ever want a woman who made more money than he did. This left Lois with a great deal of bitterness and resentment toward the idea that she had to look like a "girl" in order to get a man.

"Would you be willing to let go of some of that anger and bitterness so you could make space to explore how you want to dress, free of that influence?" I inquired.

"I think I do dress how I want to, but I will consider your idea."

I would never suggest people try to be anyone other than their authentic self. However, I pointed out that the way she was approaching this issue made it seem like she was not open to male attention. I also suspected she might be unconsciously dressing that way for spite against a mother who didn't love her the way she was. I put it to her like this: "Look, you don't need to change a thing if you don't want to, but at least work on taking the initiative and speaking to more men so they know you are open to an invitation to get to know you better."

I felt sorry for her, as I sensed by her voice and manner how lonely she was, but I knew also that she was very afraid. That fear was blocking her from opening up to changes that would make her more approachable.

She remarked, "Well, that brings me to my next point. I need you to turn me into an extrovert so I can do that."

"Okay, give me a second," I said, "so I can dust off my magic wand."

She laughed, and I asked her my usual question when someone asks for something a bit outlandish. "Why?"

"So I can fit in better and talk to men."

"Okay, I can't make you an extrovert," I explained, "nor would I want to if I could. The gift you have of enjoying focusing on your inner world for long periods of time, makes you, you. That is why you are such a successful programmer. I can help you feel more comfortable in social situations, such as speaking with men and being at parties."

We then did some hypnotherapy work I created to make social situations and dating approaches more comfortable, and Jane left much happier than when she had arrived.

Later on, she e-mailed me saying she enjoyed the session but didn't think we "clicked," so she was going to look for someone else. I wished her well and suggested a couple hypnotherapists who might be a better match.

The greatest wish I always have for my clients is that they get a better sense of how important their unique brand of human being is to the world, and that they realize they are special, whole, and complete—perfect even as they strive to heal and grow. I heard a monk once say, "God loves you just as you are, but too much to let you stay that way." I've always remembered the humor and compassion expressed in that sentence. I hope Lois received this and whatever else she needed from our session, even if we didn't continue working together.

Public Speaking, a Common Trauma

Because my office is in a part of Southern California where there are a lot of technology companies, I have had quite a few immigrants to America as my clients, particularly Indian programmers.

One programmer in particular, Raj, had only been in the United States a couple of months when he had an embarrassing incident at a company holiday party. It's important to preface this by mentioning that a lot of alcohol had been served, resulting in many of the partygoers having lost their inhibitions. This made Raj's episode worse than if there'd been a soberer crowd.

My client had a couple of drinks, and it was late in the evening. One of his female coworkers lived down the street from his house, and he asked her in front of a large group of people if he could "ride her home after the party." Everyone laughed hysterically, and Raj, who didn't have a firm grasp on the American version of English, was unaware what was so funny. The female coworker didn't laugh and politely said, "I think you mean to ask if I could give you a ride home, and yes, I can." Then, another coworker ridiculed Raj further for his error in a crude way, and everyone laughed even harder. One other person not laughing was the human resources manager, who decided it would be best if the drunken employees take cabs home separately, rather than get rides from female coworkers.

The damage was done. My client felt humiliated and traumatized by the event. In addition, the manager's insistence that he take a cab gave him the feeling the others thought of him not only as an idiot, but as a rapist as well.

Two years later, my client was working at a new job that required him to give short presentations about the status of his projects, but now he discovered he had a crippling fear of simply introducing himself to a group.

Mundane things like my client's humiliation at the office party tend to be especially traumatizing if there was an earlier, unhealed event that gets triggered by present circumstances. The person assumes the most recent occurrence caused the problem; however, the real root is often an ugly memory from childhood, giving rise to a false belief about the significance of what happened or a negative effect on the person's self-image.

It's easier to unearth those buried early memories, which are secretly undermining us, while a person is under hypnosis. In Raj's case, the significant memory was his having to solve a math problem on the chalkboard in front of the entire class and being unable to do it. The teacher berated him for his "stupidity" in front of everyone, and as a result, Raj formed an unconscious belief that he was stupid despite the fact that he went on to earn a master's degree in computer science. This belief about himself was lodged deep in his psyche, causing him to struggle speaking in front of a group.

Fortunately, through hypnotherapy, Raj was able to release those negative associations with public speaking and feel more neutral about sharing in front of others.

Interestingly, I have noted many instances of people humiliated when they are sent to the front of the classroom to do a math problem on the chalkboard. It seems this is a common traumatic event at the root of a great number of peoples' fear of public speaking. It also frequently comes up when I work with individuals on confidence issues.

Even though public speaking is often required of us as adults, so few people truly feel comfortable talking to large groups. This is a shame, given how many people have helpful and inspiring words to share. Because of the fear of public speaking, the world misses out on many creative and wise ideas.

If this is an issue for you, seek help from a hypnotherapist or join a group such as Toastmasters, where you can practice speaking in front of a group of highly supportive people who want to see you succeed. If you are a teacher, please don't play out the chalkboard scenario with your students, or they may need my help later! On the other hand, I suppose I can use the business…

A Tale of Two New Americans

In the course of one week I ended up working with two woman who had the exact same name, looked so much alike they could have been sisters, with remarkably similar childhoods, yet remarkably different adulthoods.

I have often pondered the idea of nature verses nurture, that is, the concept that a person's upbringing—being raised in a healthy, loving home, or one filled with abuse and degradation—that is, how a person is "nurtured," is the determining factor in their eventual success or failure, as opposed to the notion that "nature," the genes present in their family lineage, is the most significant influence. Speaking objectively or scientifically, we know that a person who commits murder is usually not from a family of murderers, and also that some of the most prominent people in the world came from the humblest of circumstances. I find it fascinating to see how two people from similar backgrounds can end up going in vastly different life directions.

This is well demonstrated by my two clients, Sylvia and Lucia, both first-generation Americans born in Mexico of American fathers of Hispanic descent and Hispanic mothers. Both Sylvia and Lucia had endured childhoods filled with violence against their passive and accepting mothers by fathers who as, Lucia put it, "only came around to get money and to make Mom pregnant again." Both these clients had moved to San Diego as teenagers and had spent at least some time in local high schools. Both had done all right in school, but had continued to suffer from lack of stability in their homes and, of course, money issues.

When I met Lucia, she was the mother of two young children by two different fathers, neither of whom had she married. Neither father was providing any child support. She had recently lost her job as a truck driver by getting a DUI and was currently living back at her mom's house with her two children while trying to find a new job. When she told me all this, I was surprised and also very saddened to learn that the only thing she wanted me to help her with was to lose weight so she could attract a new boyfriend. Lucia told me, "I feel like all my problems would be solved if I would just find the right guy."

I knew her plan wouldn't work, because as a child raised with domestic violence, there was little chance she would be attracted to anyone close to being "the right guy" without a serious amount of psychotherapy. I would love to have worked with her on self-esteem and confidence, and because her last two boyfriends had both been abusive, I also thought she would do better to address those wounds from the past, so she could begin adjusting her "man compass" to stop drawing in men who weren't good for her or her children.

However, Lucia objected loudly when I suggested she had bigger problems than just a few pounds. She said, "I can only afford to come this once, and I only want to work on weight loss." I explained to her that all the other life problems she was experiencing were the reason she was overeating in the first place, but I understood and respected her wishes as my client. We did as much as we could in one session, during which I guided her through a hypnotherapy process to encourage better eating habits and help her feel more comfortable in her own skin, so that she could express confidence, which is very attractive to a potential match.

She left my office happy, although I never saw her again.

By contrast, later that day I saw Sylvia, who, like Lucia, had grown up amid domestic violence with a mother who was routinely beaten up by a father who was never around, except when he was inflicting pain on someone or creating another sibling for her mother to feed.

Sylvia was working with me on two issues, sleep and confidence. She had never been able to sleep well at night, which had started in her childhood when her father would frequently come home drunk in the early hours of the morning and start beating up her mom. She and her brothers often tried to protect her mother, but she had come away with the fear that if she slept through a really bad fight, her mother might get killed by her father.

Sylvia and Lucia both relayed that as children, they had been praised for being quiet and meek, but punished if loud or complaining. This is where the similarity between these women ended.

Sylvia was a very successful executive with a master's degree from University of California San Diego—a very challenging and respectable accomplishment—as well as a happy, stable marriage to, as she put it, "one of the nicest guys on the planet." Her issue with lack of confidence was a common problem I encounter with people (mostly women) who rise to a station above others in their family. "I feel like I am still that nobody from a dirt shack in one of the poorest parts of Tijuana, and that if my coworkers figure this out, they will realize I am really a fraud."

Unlike Lucia, while Sylvia was growing up in her abusive home environment, she said, she daily vowed she would never be like her mom. "I saw what was happening, and I promised myself over and over again that I would never have a life like that." She kept that promise.

I asked her if there was anyone, a grandmother, teacher, or someone else in her family who had encouraged her and put her on the right path. She replied, "No one in my family but there was my best friend's mother, Marie." Her best friend Carrie came from a wealthy family and "she was expected to go to college," Sylvia explained. "It wasn't an option for her, so I thought, well, I won't let it be an option for me either. When she applied to a college, I applied too, thinking… why not? I got accepted to lots of places and even earned a few scholarships, but in the end I ran the numbers [she was quite good with numbers], and going to a state university made the most sense."

"Marie had a big part in this. When she got a college application for her daughter she grabbed one for me as well. She actually filled out many of them with me. When it was time for Carrie to take the SAT she registered and paid for me as well. She even paid for me to take a cram class for the exam with her daughter." Marie had told her this was because if Sylvia went then Carrie would want to go as well but Sylvia always felt it was more of a gesture of love because she believed in Sylvia. This became a major support for Sylvia.

Even though there was no money from her family for college, Sylvia had some scholarships and a small grant when she graduated from high school. She decided to go to college regardless. "I worked two jobs and had four roommates. It took me six years to earn a four-year degree, but I did it anyway because I wanted a better life for myself. After I graduated from college, I said 'f**k graduating… I'm not going to stop now,' so I applied for a master's degree program at UCSD [not an easy school to get into or graduate from, by the way]. Shockingly, I was accepted!"

Furthermore, unlike Lucia, Sylvia got help for her emotional issues. "While in college, I was given the option of some free and reduced-price counseling, so I took it. These counselors were mostly students or clinical social workers, but I had learned early on in life if someone offers you something you need for free, with no strings attached, you take it."

The counseling Sylvia participated in had a huge impact on shifting her relationships with men, and when I asked her about dating in college, she gave me an answer I have never heard before. "Oh, there was almost no dating for me while in college… I needed to focus on school and one of my eighteen jobs to pay for school. I couldn't take the chance of getting pregnant and ending up like my mom. My husband, whom I met while working on my master's degree, had to chase me to get my attention. That wasn't because I didn't like him—I really did—but my schooling and the future it would provide for me and possibly my children, was much more important than my romantic interests."

When I heard this, I honestly wished Sylvia could come and give a lecture about this to the female teenage clients I see. I even went so far as to tell her I wished she would write a book about this. However, she replied, "I am more of a numbers person. Maybe I could just talk about the numbers in someone else's book about this topic." I sincerely hope she does.

Besides being traumatized during her childhood, Sylvia felt somewhat alienated with the corporate world. "Nothing in my childhood prepared me for being looked up to and respected," she said. "Don't get me wrong—I like it—but I feel like a faker, as though I will be found out at any moment. Even though I am very good at leading a team, I still find it very hard to feel like I am the one who should be in charge. No one in my family has ever gone to college, few have finished high school—my own mother only has a sixth-grade education. I had no role models to follow, no one encouraging me, and no one expecting me to do well. Basically, I was on my own, and that is not a comfortable place to be." I hear this all the time from clients who go beyond the family norm and become successful in spite of their family's history.

People like this tell me they fear failure, although some tell me it's really more a fear of success. My favorite hypnotherapy teacher, Michele Meiche, once explained that it's actually fear of moving ahead of your family of origin. I see evidence of this almost daily in clients who come to me for help with a variety of issues.

While it could be argued that Sylvia may have been smarter than Lucia, I don't think this is true. I think both women were very smart and had a chance to succeed against very poor odds. It could also be argued that having two children and a high school education only does not make someone a loser… it is just one place in life and after all, Lucia did have a roof over her head, which is more than many in her situation can say.

Nevertheless, these two women were clearly different, and their choices made a huge impact on the generations to come. Perhaps the difference was in how they reacted to a disadvantage childhood—wanting more versus being satisfied with the status quo. Perhaps it was in their relative abilities to keep commitments they made to themselves, to be courageous enough to confront their own issues and weaknesses, to work hard even when this was challenging, to persist in the face of defeat. Perhaps it was Sylvia's good friend's mother who helped her fill out those college applications and believed in her or perhaps it was the help she got from counseling. There's no simple answer, certainly, but Sylvia's attitude and her courage to live a life that was different from the one her family envisioned for her enabled her to improve the quality of her life, while at the same time showing her future children that having a better life is always a choice, no matter what.

No matter how humble your beginnings everyone deserves the best in life, and I believe everyone is capable of greatness. It starts with deciding that you will have it no matter what, seeking help along the way, and having enough courage to go where no one around you has gone before. Love yourself enough to do what you need to do to achieve your dreams.

Woman Hating on Woman Has to Stop!

I feel like I need to close the section on confidence with a story about how women hurt each other in the workforce. A client named Karen came into my office one day with sadly a very common complaint: "I just got promoted at my job, I am the first female manager at my company and the other women at the office are saying I only got the job because I am sleeping with the owner. I am not, by the way. How do I explain that to them and gain respect?"

"You don't have to explain anything to them, you are the boss and if you aren't treated with respect you will have to handle that the way any male boss would." I'm not sure what that would involve in this particular case, but it felt good to say.

This one bothers me on so many levels but mostly because I see it a lot. I even watched it happen at a job to my boss who was our marketing director and brilliant. She was the owner's daughter and behind her back many of my coworkers complained that it was the only reason she got the job. Those of us who worked closely with her knew being the owner's daughter was the only reason she *took* the job; she could have worked anywhere, but instead she chose to help her dad turn his stumbling company around, so we could all still have jobs.

Women, I hate to call you out on this, but we must stop this behavior. We must celebrate other women getting promoted rather than looking at the hemline of their skirts and shaking our heads. We need to celebrate anyone who gets past that glass ceiling rather than trying to pull them down with mean comments about their bodies, their weight, their boyfriends, or speculating about how they got there. Frankly if a female boss does a good job I wouldn't care if they *were* dating the owner—I would consider that none of my business.

Women are more likely to hire more women into positions of power and that is what we need right now. Women are not as likely to participate in the kinds of disgusting sexual harassment behavior we have been seeing splattered all over the news. And I have yet to meet anyone who got a D**k pic from a female boss, though I guess it's still early in the day.

Look, we have all known people, both men and women, who were grossly incompetent who got promoted to positions they had no business having, but for some reason it's the women who really get criticized for this one and if women want to get ahead in this world, this is the behavior that most needs to change.

It's okay to feel a bit jealous, that's human nature, but don't let the jealously keep you from treating your new female boss with the respect she deserves and know that she just proved that with hard work, it can be possible for you too.

With Doris the key was working on her confidence, feeling comfortable with her new role as a manager, and speaking her truth no matter what, and to some extent ignoring her nay-sayers. Having said all that, I know she had a tough road ahead, tougher than most, but I considered it a huge victory to see another strong, competent woman in a position of power.

Confidence is about self-love, knowing yourself, and having respect. People who love themselves and are full of confidence are less likely to criticize others. They know who they are within themselves and don't feel the need to put others down. We all need to learn to love ourselves enough to treat everyone with respect. It truly makes the world a better place.

Chapter 10
Secondary Gain: Problems with a Purpose

What Is Secondary Gain?

For just about every problem people suffer from, there is often a secondary gain for them—some benefit they're getting from having the frequently debilitating issue. Most sufferers are unaware that their issue is even giving them a pay-off, much less what the pay-off is.

My very first experience with secondary gain was when I was working as a home health aide while going to nursing school. I noticed that a lot of my patients would do things to sabotage their recovery, such as not take their medications, eat things they weren't supposed to, and not do prescribed exercises. Since my services were far from cheap, I had trouble understanding why they wouldn't do everything they could to shorten the time they needed my help. Eventually, one patient in particular showed me the answer to that question.

Margaret was recovering from hip replacement surgery, and she required the use of a walker to get around. She had some treacherous steps in her home that were difficult to get up and down, as well as rugs on the floor that were very easy to trip over. Her family had put in some ramps, but she kept pushing them out of position. Because of this, she had to have a home health aide stay with her to help her do ordinary life chores.

One day while she was napping, I moved some of her furniture to make it easier for her to get to the bathroom, and I rolled up the carpets in her path to the bathroom so she wouldn't need as much help getting up at night. I thought she would be happy about this, since it would mean more freedom for her. I was wrong. She actually became so upset that she called her family and asked them to come over and move everything back to the way it had been. The next day, I was told not to mess with it again.

I was really stunned. Why wouldn't Margaret want to be free of having a stranger in her home at night so she could go to the bathroom? Then it occurred to me… if she could manage on her own, she wouldn't need us aides, and she would be alone again in her big house with no one to talk to. It seemed really sad to me that this vibrant old lady, who had lived a full life, was reduced to having to stunt her own healing process just to get some much-needed company and attention. At least I understood why some people weren't trying harder to get better. I never moved anyone's furniture again.

Now, in my hypnotherapy practice, I see the same thing: problems that have a pay-off for the client. Most frequently it is evident in patients that have fears/phobias, weight issues, and sports injuries that never seem to heal. Secondary gains can be a touchy subject, and I have had more than one client get very defensive when I suggested they might be getting something out of their problem. Nevertheless, I'm not doing my job if I don't (gently) tell it like I see it.

I had a client once named Stephanie who was in her late sixties and was coming to me for help with weight loss. She was only trying to lose twenty pounds and she looked great, so I was somewhat surprised she was even bothered by her weight. Stephanie told me she had struggled with her weight her entire life and that before she died, she wanted to be her ideal weight again. She had been very thin at times in her life, but it had been at least twenty-five years since she had been the weight she was trying to reach now. She expressed that she spent almost every waking moment thinking about food and feeling bad about herself and her body because of her weight. Secretly, I thought it was a shame that such a lovely woman had spent so much of her life, time, and energy trying to be at a weight her body didn't seem to want her to be. I suspected that she had low self-esteem and was using weight as a way to beat herself up out of self-hatred.

As I often do, I asked Stephanie to think about the possibility of maintaining her current weight for the rest of her life. I ask this question to many of my weight-loss clients, not only to encourage them to think differently about this issue, but also because their answer tells me a lot about where they are emotionally regarding food and their weight, often revealing their real pain point about it.

In Stephanie's case, she became very angry. "That's not even an option! You don't understand. I can never be happy at my weight! It's just not acceptable." I let her know I wasn't saying she couldn't change, but that I simply wanted her to consider that maybe her value to the world was much more than just what she weighed, and that she should consider loving herself and working on weight loss from a place of self-love rather than anger, to produce better and long-lasting results.

She left without scheduling another appointment, so I suspected Stephanie didn't like my approach. Later, I got an angry e-mail from her saying she felt I hadn't listened to her and didn't "get" how important it was to her that she lose the weight. I suspected she was really angry at herself over her body and wasn't ready to consider the idea that she, as a person, was worth more than just a number on a scale. I hoped that later, she might be able to let go worrying about those twenty pounds and learn to love herself as she was. What a sad circumstance to spend the next couple decades of her life feeling bad every time she put food in her mouth. Also, if she was using her weight as a way of beating herself up, she might not be able to get over that by simply losing weight.

From my own personal experience, when I first sought help from a hypnotherapist for my weight problem, I became protective like Stephanie, when she brought up the possibility that my being seventy pounds overweight might be serving a purpose in my life. Over the years, I've noticed that when I get defensive, it's because something is getting a little close to a pain point that I am not completely ready to address yet. I remember saying to her angrily, "No! I am getting nothing out of this. It's only causing me pain." I don't even remember her response, but I do recall being really irate at her for implying that on some level, I might be overweight on purpose.

After I calmed down a bit, which I have to admit took a while, I considered her question and actually came up with a few things that being overweight was doing for me. This realization was actually a huge turning point in my progress toward better health. For me, being overweight was the mother of all excuses for why things didn't go my way. If I was on a first date with someone and he didn't ask for a second date, instead of admitting I didn't really like the guy either or that we just hadn't clicked, I would say it was because I was overweight. If I didn't get a job I wanted, it wasn't because perhaps I wasn't qualified or wanted more money than they wanted to pay, but explained it away with my weight. Also, being "too fat" was a great excuse not to push myself to try more difficult things that would further my career, such as public speaking.

For me and, I believe, for many, many overweight people, it was simply much easier to blame any and all of my life's failing on fat, rather than having to take a closer look at why I wasn't getting what I wanted. My fat allowed me to distance myself personally—after all, my date didn't reject *me*, he rejected my fat; that employer didn't say "no" to *me*, they were just prejudiced against people my size; and of course, why bother trying something as risky as public speaking if my body wasn't presentable?

I sent an e-mail to Stephanie expressing this, but she didn't respond. As shown in this chapter's stories, finding out and confronting a problem's secondary gain can be the key to solving issues that have been hanging around for a lifetime.

I'm Terrified, but I Like It

One day, a middle-aged woman named Jackie came into my office with a fairly common problem, fear of driving. During our initial conversation, I asked her the usual questions about when this fear started, etc., and got the typical answers. "I have always been a bit uncomfortable with driving, but one day someone cut me off and then *flipped me off*, and I suddenly found myself having a panic attack. I got so freaked out by the experience and the possibility that I might pass out and die, that I haven't been able to make myself drive on the freeway since. My father was always afraid of driving, so I may have picked it up from him."

Jackie explained that she was a homemaker and mother of five children, a few of whom are now teenagers. This issue had been going on since her teenagers were small children.

I asked her how she was able to cope with this issue and get around with that many children. "When they were really young, I had a neighbor who liked to drive, so we would go run errands together. But I couldn't always count on her, so I figured out how to get around without using the freeway [trust me… this is no small task in Southern California!]. Other times, I saved things that required a freeway drive for when my husband came home from work, but he is tired after a long day and doesn't really like it when I do that. As my children grew up and started driving themselves, I started taking one of them with me to run errands."

Over the years of working with people who are afraid to drive on the freeway, I have learned that many of these people are experts at knowing bus schedules, back roads, and train schedules to get them just about anywhere. If you ever need directions about how to get somewhere, ask someone who's afraid to drive on the freeway. They can draw you a great map!

Since Jackie seemed to have created a system that worked for her, I asked her why she had come to me. "Well, my kids and my husband are starting to get really impatient with me, and sometimes it would be nice to be able to visit a friend once in a while without having to get a ride." She added, "I don't know why they get upset at me. I do everything for them."

I caught the resentment in her voice, so I asked her more about that. It turns out she was a very hands-on mother and did almost all the cooking and cleaning for the entire family, which with seven people and several of these teenagers, is *a lot* of housework.

We worked for several sessions and used a variety of processes, but with limited success. At this point, I began to think there might be secondary gain involved. I suspected that on some level, Jackie liked having her kids and husband do the driving, so I pressed on in that direction.

Initially, I tried asking Jackie just to think of what she might be getting out of this, but she became a bit defensive (always a sign I am on the right track) and said she couldn't come up with anything. Under hypnosis, I addressed the part of her that was scared of what she might be getting out of it. She told me that in her life, she takes care of everyone else around her—the kids, her husband, and parts of her husband's business. Driving her places was the one thing in her life that her family had to do for her. Part of her was craving being taken care of... this was something she felt like she really needed. Having this fear became the excuse for not driving, which she admitted was something that she hadn't liked doing even before developing her phobia.

In session we talked about other ways she might get that need met, including working on having her teenaged children do more of the household chores, which they were more than capable of doing, as well as doing more things for herself. I also suggested she have a talk with her husband about his being more loving and affectionate.

Jackie did follow through with some of the things I suggested, but admitted she was having a hard time asking her kids to take on more responsibilities at home. According to her belief system, being a good mother meant taking care of all those things for her husband and children. I suspected she also didn't want to have to work outside the home, and if she didn't have so much housework, she might feel unable to justify not having a job. In the end, Jackie's fear of freeway driving improved, but she wound up as a no-show for her last two sessions. It is many times the unfortunate reality that even when people are aware of the secondary gain they're receiving from a problem, they are not ready or completely willing to give up that pay-off.

My Big Fat Revenge

I had been working with a woman named Irene on weight loss for a couple of months, and she had experienced some success, but not as much as she wanted. She was starting to get frustrated with herself, the process, and even me. Like a lot of people trying to lose weight, she would go along for a while doing all the right things. Then, she would give into temptation and have a candy bar, followed by a second, a third, and finally, "Forget it! I'll just eat what I want." A full-on binge for the next few hours or days would follow.

As you can imagine, this was hugely frustrating to Irene, and it was interfering with her reaching the goal of creating the body and life she wanted.

During our next session, I hypnotized her and guided her to connect with the part of her that was hungry all the time. I asked this part of her if she really wanted to lose weight.

The response was, "No!"

"Why not?" I asked her.

"Because I am angry at my husband for being so mean to me about my weight. I want him to love me as I am," came her reply.

I then asked the part of her that didn't want to lose the weight if it would be willing to set aside the anger toward her husband, so that Irene could achieve her goals.

The answer was a very strong and forceful, "No!"

Again, I asked, "Why not?"

"Because then my husband will win, and I don't want him to win. I want to get back at him for cheating on me."

Whoa. This was the first I had heard about cheating! I had had several sessions with Irene, and when I asked, as I always do when it comes to weight loss, how her relationship with her husband was going, I would always get a rather evasive, "Fine … everything's fine." If I pressed for more information, she would usually reply with more "fine's" before quickly changing the subject. I had suspected there was more to the story, but if she didn't want to talk about it, she didn't have to. Obviously, though, it makes it much harder to get to the heart of any issue when clients leave important things out of the conversation.

While she was still under hypnosis, I explained to her, "Irene, this is about you and what you want. Would you be willing to set your anger aside, so you can have better health?"

Her answer: "My health is fine."

Okay, I struck out with that. I then tried another approach and said to her, "What would make you become willing to set aside your anger so you can have an amazing body?"

She replied, "I already have an amazing body. My husband is the only one who thinks I'm fat."

I actually liked these answers! My client was perhaps fifteen pounds overweight, and I had already suggested several times that she looked great the way she was. Nonetheless, she had insisted she needed to lose weight. I finally learned that she thought she should lose weight because her husband had told her the reason he cheated was because she was fat, and he no longer found her attractive. So now, part of Irene didn't want to let go of the weight as a way of getting back at him.

Next, I asked her, "Would you be willing to find another way to express your anger toward your husband so that you can be allowed to lose the weight if you choose to, either now or in the future?"

At last, she said, "Yes."

We then completed a process where, with the help of her former saboteur, we created new habits that would help her toward the body and life she wanted.

When Irene came out of hypnosis, I asked her why she hadn't mentioned the cheating issue before. She admitted that when I had asked before, she hadn't been ready to talk about the situation, which had happened recently. She had been in denial, and hadn't decided if she wanted to push him to try marriage counseling together or end their already troubled relationship. I suggested she at least consider marriage counseling, so she could feel better about leaving if that was her ultimate decision. I gave her a referral to someone I knew.

After a few months, Irene sent me an e-mail saying they had decided to separate and were headed toward divorce. In the end, she lost the weight once she started looking at her emotions and addressing her anger, rather than stuffing it down with food. For Irene, finally being able to admit to herself that she was infuriated with her husband for what he had done proved to be the secret to losing weight and keeping it off.

I ran into Irene recently and was stunned by the giant rock on her wedding finger and by how healthy she looked. "You got married!" "Yes," she said, "to a wonderful man who treats me with respect. We are so happy, we truly are each other's soul mates." She was absolutely glowing. I was excited for her. I wish people could see that on the other side of a bad situation like an unpleasant marriage to a cheater there might be a beautiful relationship with lots of love just waiting for you to be free of the old. Everyone deserves to be happy and sometimes the key to something good really is getting rid of something bad.

"Help! I Accidentally Made Myself Impotent"

One of my first experiences with hypnotherapy, before I had entered the field myself, was during my employment as a health coach at a company that made natural, hormone-balancing products. Most of the calls I handled were from women looking for help with hot flashes or PMS, but on this occasion, it was a male caller suffering the unfortunate, all-too-common problem of sexual dysfunction. As he put it, "I accidentally made myself impotent, and I need your help."

As I talked to this man, I learned he was deeply religious. In his faith, it was considered infidelity to even think about a woman who was not his wife in a sexual way. Unfortunately, in his occupation as a commercial photographer, he took pictures of women wearing little to no clothing, and even though he was married, these women would flirt with him, making it impossible not to think of them sexually. Since he didn't want to spend eternity in a very hot place (to his way of thinking), he created an interesting yet equally destructive way of dealing with this problem. He put on a lot of weight. At the time I was speaking with him, he weighed almost four hundred pounds and had not been able to have sex for some time.

None of his tremendous weight gain had been done on a conscious level, so for a long time he couldn't figure out what had caused his obesity and performance issues. One of his friends had suggested hypnotherapy to him, and under hypnosis it was revealed that he was creating these problems as a way of saving both his marriage and his soul.

I had a stack of brochures for various hypnotherapy schools on my desk at the time, and I couldn't resist asking him about his experiences with the hypnotherapist. "Well, after a few sessions," he told me, "she hypnotized me one day and asked, 'What are you getting out of having these problems?' Saving my marriage was the first thing that came to mind. It seemed ridiculous at the time, because in reality, it was making my marriage worse, but in a different way." He had created a real, physical issue as a way to solve an emotional one.

This is an excellent example of how our unconscious mind works. It looks at the bigger problem and tries to solve it, not noticing that it created another problem as a result of the solution. It's a bit like a dark fairytale in which the main character's wish is granted, but at some very regrettable cost, like a man granted the ability to be invisible, but when he uses it to spy on people, hears them saying bad things about him behind his back.

I spoke with the photographer again several months later, and he told me that with the help of hypnotherapy, he had made a different decision about how he would solve this problem, one that would allow him to lose the weight and be healthy. Eventually, he was able to fix the hormonal imbalance, lose weight, and return to normal sexual function. His marriage was intact, and he didn't have to give up a career he loved. All of this started when he stopped focusing on his symptoms (weight gain, impotence) and instead addressed the underlying problem. It's easy to lose sight of what's really going on with us—what we're deriving by clinging to some bad habit or issue—when we're only focusing on the painful consequences of that issue.

If this applies to you regarding some troubling behavior you can't seem to shake, try asking yourself, "How am I benefiting from this problem? What am I getting out of this?" Your first reaction will likely be an angry, "Nothing! This is all bad." Go deeper. Play devil's advocate and look at issues like, "Am I getting much-needed attention because I have this problem? Am I managing to avoid something I don't want to deal with because of this difficulty?" Being honest with yourself may not automatically resolve the issue, but you will be much closer to an answer than you were before. Here is where you can begin to address the core issues rather than just putting a bandage on surface wounds.

Chapter 11
Anxiety: The Mother of All Symptoms

How Do You Spell A-N-X-I-E-T-Y?

Stress, anxiety, and worry—or as I call them, the Trifecta of Trouble—are what drive a huge percentage of my business. In fact, around the holidays, about 90 percent of my clients are there because of these symptoms. Although anxiety is the human response to a problem, rather than the problem itself, there are differences in its frequency and intensity among individuals. Some people seem to be naturally "wound a little tighter" than others and more prone to having long-term anxiety issues.

I have something of a reputation for developing a particularly effective set of hypnotherapy techniques to address these issues, with the result that after I work with one person, they often send their friends to see me also! Of course, this doesn't hurt my feelings one bit…

It's been my observation over the years that for many people, medications help, but in my opinion, not as well as hypnotherapy and practice of daily meditation. However, I am not a physician, so take my words with a grain of salt. It has been my experience that hypnotherapy is so effective on issues involving anxiety, that it should be tried before agreeing to medication. It pains me to see so many people suffering with difficulties so readily addressed through hypnosis.

If you're suffering in the "Trifecta," get help in some form. You're too important to the world and the people who love you to endure something so treatable.

Two Programmers, One Douche Bag

I hate to say it, but often, peoples' bad behavior is great for my business. A large technology company located around where I practice happened to employ a terrible manager, who was stressing out his staff so much that several of them wound up coming to me for anxiety relief. This was the fortunate part, as treating anxiety is one of my particular specialties. In spite of working with a total of five of this manager's employees, I never actually heard his real name because these clients only ever called him "The D-Bag." I suppose I should send him a "thank-you" note for all the business he unknowingly sent my way, but because I don't feel good about getting clients this way, I'll hold off on that.

It started with just one of the programmers on his team, Jeffrey, a very tense, stressed-out senior engineer in his early thirties who had a master's degree in computer science. His severe anxiety at work began the minute he walked in the doors of the building and lasted until long after he left, when he would then struggle, usually unsuccessfully, to fall asleep at night. Like many of my anxiety clients, Jeffrey also suffered severe acid reflux disease—which often goes hand-in-hand with tension overload—so in addition to experimenting with some anti-anxiety medications, he also used anti-reflux pills, plus roll after roll of chewable antacids.

The job itself was stressful, with tight deadlines that had him working late and on weekends, but that was nothing new for Jeffrey, and because he actually really enjoyed what he did, that wasn't the trouble. The real stress came from the D-Bag, a recently promoted, new manager who was belligerent and constantly yelling at his staff, almost all of whom were male. As Jeffrey put it, "It's hard to imagine this, but I sit at the desk in front of his office, and I see grown men come out of there crying after being yelled at, usually for something that isn't entirely their fault. This guy knows just which buttons to push to make his employees feel really bad about themselves." The worst part, according to Jeffrey, was that this manager wasn't very technically oriented and would make ridiculous demands, some of which were not physically possible, from his employees.

My client explained a particular problem he and the twenty other members of the team were having. "He has gotten it in his head that this huge project we are doing needs to be coded in a particular language, one that is entirely wrong for something this size and will cause the software to be unstable, with lots of crashes as we get further along. We have all told him this many times, but he just yells that we are lazy and stupid, then suggests we all learn Hindi if we want to keep our jobs because he's going to farm this off to India if we don't do as we are told! So we proceed toward certain disaster, which could result in our whole team getting laid off anyway."

During our hypnotherapy sessions, Jeffrey and I went through various stress reduction processes to help him deal with the situation at work, as well as some work to help him see that his boss's aggressiveness was a reflection of this manager's own insecurities, not Jeffrey's performance. It worked so well for Jeffrey that over the next few weeks, four of his coworkers came to me for the same basic issue. This was great, as I felt very positive about my apparent success with Jeffrey and the others reaching out for help. However, it posed a particular problem I had not anticipated.

With Jeffrey and his coworkers, I did variations of a certain process where I had all of them imagine their manager as a barnyard animal or some other kind of silly character, one that made them laugh instead of becoming stressed. I then had them imagine a smaller version of their boss who spoke in a high, squeaky voice, so that rather than get anxious when they heard it, they would find it funny and laugh.

This is a highly effective process that I have used with probably one hundred or more clients over the years, but never before with people who worked and attended business meetings together. I soon found out why this wasn't a good idea. One day, the D-Bag called a meeting with his entire staff. After telling everyone to be on time, he showed up fifteen minutes late and immediately started yelling. The first words out of his mouth to a room full of talented engineers, most of whom had either a PhD or master's degree in computer science or another area of technology, was that they were all "a bunch of f***-ing morons." My clients from the team were in the room, and all of them started laughing at once. As soon as they started, everyone else joined in, and soon the room was full of a bunch of laughing men who were not paying any attention to the manager in front yelling. He literally got laughed out of his own meeting.

My clients liked it, but I know that's the kind of thing that gets people fired, so I have since adjusted that process a bit.

Very soon after that, one of the members of the team took everyone's complaint to one of the company's vice presidents (the D-Bag's boss) as well as a financial estimate he had made of how much it would cost the company to do this project incorrectly. After that, the D-Bag got "reassigned" to another department. The person who had spoken with the VP said that the higher-up didn't seem to care about the stress this manager put on his staff, but was more concerned when the team member brought up the financial consequences and likelihood that when the project failed, everyone associated with it—including the VP—would likely get fired. I found it interesting that it took someone pointing out a very specific and very large dollar amount lost to get a company to do the right thing. This is a sad demonstration of self-interest taking precedence over the suffering of others ... but it worked to get rid of a bad manager!

Stress and anxiety are tough issues because there are both physical and emotional components. To some extent, feeling anxious is a habit. Obviously, we all have issues in our lives that cause us stress, but to respond to that stress with feelings of anxiety is actually a habit. And just like any habit, it can be unlearned. If you struggle with anxiety in any of its many forms, my experience is that it is one of the most quickly and easily treated symptoms using hypnotherapy. My question is, why suffer when you don't have to?

You Should Be Mad!

I often work with couples on similar yet separate issues. Usually it's the wife who comes in first for some problem, and after she discovers that therapeutic hypnosis is both effective and not some kind of voodoo, the husband comes in regarding the problem, from his end of it.

This case was no exception. I had seen Pia a week earlier for confidence and stress-related issues, and a week later, her husband, Sadar, came in for his own difficulties with anxiety. Pia and Sadar were both programmers who had met at college. Though both Indian, Pia had been born in this country, whereas her husband had grown up in India and had only been in the United States for about ten years.

I asked Sadar to explain what he thought was causing his anxiety, and I got an unusual answer. "Frankly, I can't seem to get past the resentment I have toward my employer and my bosses. You see, my wife and I started at the company on the same day, went to the same college, got the same degree, and have the same job, but I make more money than she does… a lot more. She gets what I think you in this country call 'lady bucks.'" Under other circumstances, I would have laughed at his reference to a very funny, yet sadly true, segment done on the *Last Week Tonight with John Oliver* show on HBO the week earlier, where John Oliver referred to the 76 cents that women get for every dollar a man gets, as "Lady Bucks." However, Sadar was not smiling, and it isn't funny when it's happening for real, right in front of you.

"Out of curiosity," I asked him, "how much of a difference are we talking about here? The equivalent of a new car? Is it actually 76 percent of what you make?"

He replied, "I don't think about it in terms of a car because that's not what we would buy. More like a year of college at UCSD [around $26,000]. That's how much my family is being robbed by our employer, and I am mad. Don't get me wrong … our children will go to college, even if that means my wife and I have to work four jobs each, but it really isn't fair, and I am having a hard time not being resentful."

I had heard this same story told many times by very angry women in relation to their male coworkers, but I had never actually heard a man complain about it. Certainly, I had never encountered a man who saw the bigger picture of his whole family being cheated by this injustice. Sadar went on, "You in this country talk about freedom and fairness and justice, but yet you allow this kind of practice to happen in almost every company in every part of the country, and I don't see anyone protesting it. People aren't marching in the streets over this issue. Why is that?"

I found this question difficult to answer, and it bothered me for many reasons, the greatest of which was that Sadar was pointing out an unfortunate truth. "Sadar, I hate to say this, but as women, we have become used to it, to some extent. That doesn't mean it doesn't make us angry, and that we won't complain about it when it is right in our face, but no one wants to take on that kind of ongoing fight. Also, the truth is, it usually doesn't go well for those who do fight it. That doesn't mean we shouldn't protest, but it's one reason we don't."

Sadar told me that my answer was the reason he and his wife, who actually had a pretty good legal case against their company, had decided not to battle them. "They could easily come up with some reason why she doesn't make as much as me, and our lawyer said it would be a really hard case to prove."

During our hypnotherapy session, we did some work on anxiety and letting go of anger. Sadar was smiling and seemed to be feeling better when he left my office.

Now, though, *I* was angry! Sadar's story had triggered my own personal frustration with every employer I'd had where I knew I was being robbed of that 25 percent as well as promotions I deserved, but which had been given to my male counterparts instead. Then, of course, my anger surfaced about an obscene phone call I had received earlier that day, during which I asked a prospective client *when* he would like to come in, and he told me *what* he would like to come in. At the time, I had laughed it off, but now I wondered if, as people on this planet, we were laughing off too many things. Why weren't more women upset about this disparity in equal pay for equal work? Why should a family with two incomes lose nearly 25 percent of one provider's salary? And why weren't more men upset about this as well? In our supposedly progressive country, why should this happen even once at a company, with no consequences?

Oddly enough, two weeks later I got an e-mail from Sadar about a different and interesting side effect of making less money. It turned out that after I had seen him, the company had a big layoff. No one was certain how they decided who stayed and who was laid off, but it looked like the accounting department had simply gone down the employee list, taken a look at the salaries, and gotten rid of the highest-paid personnel. Thus, Sadar was let go, and Pia kept her job. To be fair, it could be argued that Sadar's resentful attitude had factored into their choice. Fortunately for Sadar, he was able to get a better job for a higher salary at a neighboring company.

As a result of my work with Pia and Sadar, I had to ask myself why Sadar, a first-generation American male, had actually been more upset about unequal treatment of women than I had been. It brought to mind how women in general are socialized not to make waves. Also, I realized how easy it is to ignore something just because you see it all the time, even if that thing is immoral and harmful. As a result, I raised my rates the very next week—not by a lot, mind you, but I certainly didn't want to be the one denying myself a fair salary. I didn't get one single complaint, which made me think I should've done it much sooner!

Is there something in your life that is not right that you are just brushing by and ignoring? Overlooking because you see it all the time and have now become blind to it? Perhaps it is time to take a closer look, make a change, and heal it. And who knows, resolving it just might get you more money!

A Great Dane Is Not a Great Service Dog

Olivia was a former soldier who came to me for help with confidence and anxiety, two issues that coexist so often in people that my treatment usually addresses both things, even if the client only mentions one. Olivia had recently completed a job training program and was looking for a position. This meant going on job interviews, which are as nerve-wracking as first dates, except that if it doesn't go well, you may not be able to pay your rent later. It's not an easy process for anyone, but there's extra pressure for someone who only has military career experience. Olivia's military experience had been very stressful, but it hadn't required a lot of job interviews.

To make matters worse, Olivia happened to suffer from post-traumatic stress disorder (PTSD) and needed to bring her service dog with her whenever she went out in public. She feared this would look bad to a potential employer and make it harder to get a job, and unfortunately, I thought this was a realistic fear.

She asked me if bringing the dog to our hypnotherapy session would be a problem, and naturally I said "no," that I would be very happy to see her and her companion.

What Olivia didn't know was that I have my own history with dogs. In fact, as I mentioned earlier in this book, my fear of dogs is what got me into hypnotherapy in the first place. I often tell about my attack by a pit bull, but the whole story is that I was actually bitten three times—first, by my great-grandfather's Great Dane, Stormy (yes, that's right… a Great Dane), a usually gentle giant who, for some reason, took a real dislike to me (trust me, it was mutual), and second, by another typically nonthreatening dog, a black Labrador Retriever. The third time was the charm—the pit bull—and that's when the fear really got anchored deep inside me.

I am more comfortable being around dogs now, but I won't lie. They are not my favorite animal, especially Great Danes. You can imagine my surprise when Olivia showed up with a large, pretty Great Dane. The dog was huge and very hard to miss.

Of course, Olivia's session was about her, not me, but I bring me to the session as well, and it was difficult to not flash back on Papa's big, mean Great Dane taking a chunk out of my leg when I was three. But I set the memory aside to help my client. This dog was mild and extremely well trained, never left Olivia's side, and responded to her commands instantly.

As with most of my "confidence and anxiety" clients, we talked about what Olivia wanted to achieve that she felt she could not. I asked questions to get a better idea of what was driving her lack of confidence and causing her to feel anxious. In her case, the fear of having a panic attack at any moment led her to feeling less confident in public.

When Olivia was in the military, she had been trained to be alert and watchful, always assessing her environment for anything that seemed unusual in the event of a potential threat. This hypervigilance had saved her life on several occasions while she was in the armed forces. However, she was home now and found herself unable to relax while in public. She told me she'd catch herself examining peoples' backpacks to see if they seemed unusually heavy, which in the military was indicative of a possible bomb. She would notice someone wearing extra heavy clothing on a warm day, or a car with only one person in it riding too low to the ground, which in the Middle East were potential signs of explosives. When Olivia saw these things back here, she became nervous, as though she was still in the service.

My work with her consisted of reminding her psyche that she was now "off duty," and it was okay to allow someone else to take over the job of protection. We rechanneled the confidence she had had while she was in the military to a new career. Also, I gave her a list of the most common job interview questions and, under hypnosis, had her practice interviews with positive outcomes. This reinforced confidence that her interviews would go well, thereby decreasing the scariness around that situation. I strongly recommended she apply for and go on job interviews for jobs she didn't want, just so she could get more comfortable with interviewing.

A few weeks later, Olivia called to reschedule her appointment because she had gotten a job! Her new company was happy to have both her and her lovely service dog.

Every client helps me learn, sometimes even things about myself. Olivia taught me about the gifts that well-trained service dogs bring to their owners. At the beginning of our sessions, I would ask Olivia if I could say "hi" to her dog, and she would give Fido (*okay, seriously?*) the release command, sending her over to me. Before I'd even realize what was happening, Fido would give me one long lick on the face, from the bottom of my chin to the top of my hairline. Eww… yet, so cute! And with that, I finally made peace with Great Danes.

Through working with Olivia (and Fido), I realized how important service dogs are to their owners. When out and about, be aware that people with service dogs really need these animals to stay on duty. Children should be instructed to treat service dogs along these lines.

When I asked Olivia about her choice of a Great Dane, she told me she wished she had picked something more frightening. "I love my dog, and I am glad I got her. But when I am out in public, little children see Fido and come running up to her screaming, 'Oh, what a cute doggie!' It's this running up to me that triggers my anxiety and makes me uncomfortable. Next time, I'm getting a pit bull." She said this jokingly, although I'm not 100 percent sure she was kidding. I have actually been told pit bulls do make really good service dogs so maybe it's a good choice for her.

The Artist Trying to Be an Insurance Agent

I received a call from an insurance agent friend of mine, Kerry, to schedule an appointment on behalf of her daughter, who was working at the family insurance business and having trouble achieving her sales numbers. My friend felt her daughter, Michelle, was sabotaging her own success, which is a common problem. I used to sell insurance myself and did quite well with it. In fact, my experience in sales prior to becoming a hypnotherapist has given me a knack for helping clients overcome sales blocks. I was more than happy to work with Michelle.

I don't usually make house calls, but Michelle lived four houses away from a family member I was visiting. When she asked for a Saturday appointment, I offered to come over instead. I was glad I did, because as soon as I walked into her home, I noticed the walls were covered floor to ceiling with some of the most beautiful artwork I have ever seen.

"Wow! Who is the artist?" I marveled.

Michelle smiled and replied, "It's me. I painted all this and a whole lot more. My house is overflowing with my art."

I was stunned. Her work was so amazingly good, I had to ask, "If you can do this, why would you want to be an insurance agent?"

"It's complicated," she told me. I thought, *I'll bet it's complicated! That sounded like an understatement.*

Michelle explained that the family business needed her, and her mom had been pressuring her to get a "real job," since selling her art had not brought money in the past. She wanted to go to graphic design school, so she could turn her art into logo designs, book covers, and other projects she thought would be fun to work on. I knew that Michelle was already a part-time college student, and I asked her why she was not already taking graphic design classes.

"Well, Mom pays for college," she said, "but she won't pay for those 'waste of time' classes." I knew Kerry was worried about Michelle's long-term financial stability, but I could also see Michelle needed to find her own way in the world.

I strongly suggested she let the insurance job be the "rent payer," while using her extra time and energy to pursue her creative ambitions, even if that meant making sacrifices and finding creative ways to pay for college on her own. If she really needed to, I felt like she could negotiate with her mom to pay for graphic design classes along with some business classes. This seemed like a helpful compromise.

During our session, we worked on increasing Michelle's feelings of confidence in herself and her ability to ask for what she needed, in addition to finding creative solutions for any potential difficulties that might arise while she tried to balance art, a job, and college all at once. When I left, she seemed happier and much more energized than when I had arrived.

I did not hear from Michelle for several years after that. One day, I went to a local art fair, and I found a booth with some of her marvelous pieces. She wasn't there, but someone else was selling her art and told me she was doing great. I felt really happy that this talented artist had pursued her passion.

Panic Attack with the Boss

Rachel was in her thirties and worked as a company sales representative. One day, her male boss called her into his office, something he never did. She went in fearing the worst. But before he could say a word, his phone rang, and he had to take it. "Stay," he told Rachel. "This will only take a second, and shut the door." The entire scenario forewarned something bad about to happen.

The phone call dragged on for more than a couple minutes, and Rachel began to stew about what was to come. She described feeling like she was a kid and her dad was about to punish her. In fact, her dad had made her wait—sometimes in his office—while he made a big show of finding a wooden paddle to spank her with when she had done something he didn't like. As more time passed sitting across from her boss, Rachel became more and more anxious, to the point of tipping into a full-on panic attack. Panic attacks can manifest with a variety of symptoms. In Rachel's case, she started hyperventilating and practically ran from his office into the bathroom to calm down.

When she came back, she made up an excuse about having to run to the bathroom for an "intestinal event you wouldn't want the details of," so she didn't have to explain her odd behavior.

It turned out that Rachel's boss had called her into his office to tell her she was doing a good job and getting a raise. He didn't want everyone in the office to hear she was getting a raise because others had recently asked for more money and been turned down.

However, after this incident, Rachel realized she had a problem. Issues left over from her abusive childhood, which she had been successfully ignoring for the most part, were surfacing again. She was finding it impossible to keep pushing her feelings down, and it was apparent that she had to face those feelings and heal her childhood wounds in order to move forward in the present.

While Rachel was coming in for help with panic attacks, we were also addressing her weight. Eating had been Rachel's primary coping method, but that was no longer working for her either. She hadn't realized the root cause of her overeating was her abusive childhood. When we started working on these old traumas, not only did her panic attacks stop, but she lost weight and gained a great deal of confidence. She reported her whole life turned around as a result of that one upsetting event at the office.

Rachel said, "That panic attack was one of the best things that ever happened to me because it forced me to do the work of healing that I needed to do, but had spent enormous effort avoiding."

Many people experience similar events, but not everyone has the courage to look deeper. Rachel was one of the brave ones who did the work it takes to look at the underlying reasons causing her panic attacks, emotional overeating, and lack of confidence in herself.

Sometimes upsetting, even traumatizing, events force us to face feelings we would much rather avoid. Like a hideously wrapped gift, they become a catalyst for healthy change, helping us dismantle old ways that no longer work and allowing us to create new ways that are effective. The tools we learn to use to deal with all of life's situations and challenges, as well as new ways of thinking and acting, provide a foundation for building lives filled with satisfaction, self-esteem, and purpose.

The Golden Handcuffs

"I have severe anxiety and I don't want to have to take medication, but I will if I don't get help," said my new client, Larry. I get this type of call about three times per week, and it's been my experience that nine times out of ten, the culprit is either work or relationship troubles. In Larry's case, it was a little of both, but mostly work.

He told me, "I am having troubles with my girlfriend. We used to get along so great. Now we fight all the time. She says my work stress is making me 'emotionally unavailable,' and that I am distant. This causes her to focus more on her work, so now I feel like *she* is distant."

Regarding his work situation, Larry spent about thirty minutes describing in great detail exactly how miserable and boring his job had become. According to him, he wasn't challenged at all anymore and could basically do the job in his sleep. "I am a project manager for a technology company and have two people under me. For the past year, work has been slow, and we haven't had a new project in a long time. My job has been mostly about maintaining our old projects." This maintenance work was anything but a challenge for Larry.

"About a month ago," he went on, "I had to have an operation and was out of the office for three weeks. They don't know this, but when I got back, it took me a total of three hours to catch up— seriously, three hours! If the owners of the company knew how little I had to do, I would have been gone a long time ago. I ask for more work, but there isn't any, so I sit around staring at my computer screen." Larry was obviously highly intelligent, so for him, this was basically torture.

I asked him why he didn't just find another job, although because I've heard this same story a few times before, I knew the only difference in Larry's answer might be the dollar amount. I was still shocked when he told me, "130K per year and with no college degree." Whoa! When you threw in the fact that he had hefty monthly child support and alimony commitments, you had the makings of a lovely pair of golden handcuffs.

I knew from experience that Larry's particular job usually required a college degree, so I asked him, "How did you get that job with no college degree?" I was genuinely curious.

"Here's the thing," he replied. "I got hired about ten years ago as a beginning level programmer. I was self-taught and used to build websites for a living, so I managed to get hired. As the years went by, I kept getting promoted. I'm good with people, very organized, and remarkably good at what I do, but I never finished my degree. They kept moving me up anyway, and now I'm way past where my education level would normally take me. I'm afraid if I leave this job, no one else will give me anywhere near the salary I make now. I have to make those child support and alimony payments, don't forget."

I suggested, "If you really think this is an issue, why not go back to college and get it?"

"At my age?!" Larry exclaimed. "No." Since he appeared to be in his mid-thirties, younger than I am, I had difficulty not laughing a bit at that response, especially since people Larry's age were going back to school to get advanced degrees in record numbers. If he really wanted to, he could easily find a local school with a schedule that would work well for him. Because I happen to work with a lot of software engineers, I knew many of them were doing just that… getting master's degrees from local colleges in their spare time. However, it was pretty clear that Larry really didn't want to do this.

I strongly suggested he consider three options, but ideally a bit of all of them. The first was to go back to school and take some challenging classes. I added, "It sounds like you have time during work hours to do homework, so why not?" The second idea was to start his own business. "Come up with an idea for an app, or several apps, put them out there, and see if anything sells. That wouldn't cost you anything, and it would probably be really fun. Plus, if anything does take off, you really will be free." My last suggestion was to update his resume and work on finding another job.

Although many jobs say they require a degree, sometimes even a master's degree, I know from personal experience and listening to clients that in many professions, good, hard-working employees can be really hard to find. Some companies will pay a premium for the right person, degree or not. My own husband interviews engineers for his job and told me, "I don't even look at the resume anymore… it's all lies anyway. I give the candidate a problem and see if they know how to solve it. That's all I really care about."

Larry left my office happy and with a renewed sense of hope. Several weeks and a few more sessions later, he came in all smiles. "I have to show you something," he told me. He gave me a website address, and what popped up was the makings of a gorgeous site with "Coming Soon" across the page. He had come up with an idea for a business that he could do in his spare time, and he was excited and motivated. Best of all, his anxiety had almost completely gone away. "I am using all that energy I used to use on feeling anxious to work on my project. I feel so much happier now than before."

Larry's relationship with his girlfriend had also improved, although it did look like they were going to be parting ways because he had begun to realize that they wanted different things in life. "She is a bit desperate to have children, and quite frankly, I feel done and don't want anymore. It's sad, but I am feeling like we aren't a match after all." As a practitioner, I was glad to see him coming to that conclusion from a place of peace rather than conflict, which would make for a much better and healthier transition.

Intelligent people need to be challenged, and this seems especially true for scientists and engineers. If your job doesn't give you the challenge you want, consider changing employers, going back to school to start work toward a new career, or creating a side business. These days, a laptop and Internet connection are just about all you need to start something new.

Chapter 12
Fails and Epic Fails

Transgender Bathroom Fail

A few years ago, I had my first transgender client. The paperwork I received online gave the name Bob, but my appointment was with Sheila. I simply figured a woman had scheduled the appointment for her husband. When a beautiful, well-dressed woman showed up with a slight five o'clock shadow and a giant Adam's apple, I thought, "This person was born a man... that's cool."

Sheila came in for something ordinary—fear of public speaking. She was so flamboyant, however, that I was a bit surprised she had the same issues most people have about public speaking. As is often the root of this fear, Sheila had been humiliated in front of her classmates as a child, working at the blackboard and laughed at for answering incorrectly. I truly wish teachers would reconsider this teaching technique! While the resulting trauma means more business for me, I would much prefer our children have a healthy, wholesome educational experience that inspires their confidence and the sharing of their gifts.

Sheila left feeling better, and we booked a second session. At the end of the session, Sheila asked to use the restroom. In my ignorance, I directed her to the men's restroom (this was before Caitlyn Jenner, who helped us all understand transgender issues better). That's when I saw angry Sheila. "Hey, show some respect! When a person presents themselves as a woman, you treat them as a woman."

I was stunned and sputtered, "I am sorry. I honestly didn't know."

"Well, now you do. Tell all your friends," Sheila said firmly.

Sheila, wherever you are, this is me telling all my friends! I was glad Sheila came in. I am now less ignorant, and she helped me to see the world through her eyes. And for that I am truly grateful she came in.

I Like Women's Panties

A prospective client found me on Yelp.com, and he wanted help with what he called "gender confusion." He told me, "I'm not gay, but I really like wearing my wife's panties. Since I travel a lot for work, and I often share a room with a coworker, it's becoming a real problem." I explained to him that if he were gay, there's nothing wrong with that, nor is it wrong to wear women's underwear. He replied, "I know that, but it's embarrassing because I am not gay." In my ignorance, I assumed this was a gay or lesbian issue, and so I referred him to a friend of mine who specializes in working with gays and lesbians. Oops…

But when I called my friend to let her know this man might call, I got an angry response from her. "You do know that a man liking women's underwear does not automatically make him gay, right?"

"Um…" I was at a loss. "I guess that's what he was trying to say, and I wasn't hearing it. Well, I really didn't know how to help him, so I sent him your way. I guess I shouldn't have told him I was sending him to a gay and lesbian specialist."

"No, you probably shouldn't have."

I have a couple of gay members in my family and have nothing but love and respect for them. Because both these incidents happened in the same week I realized, like most people, I still had a big dose of ignorance to overcome. My solution was to call a local gay/lesbian/ transgender questioning group.

"Hello, I am calling because I need a bit of help with some ignorance."

"Whose?" the operator asked.

"Mine." We met every week for a month.

Big, Black, Scary Man

One of my friends who is the same shade of Norwegian white that I am sent her husband, whom I had never met, to see me for an appointment. When the receptionist buzzed me to let me know my client was in the waiting room, I walked in, but the only person there was a large, well over six-foot-tall, African American man with dreadlocks. He stood up, extended his hand, and said, "You must be Jill." My surprise must have shown on my face. "Am I not what you expected?"

No, he isn't what I expected, I thought. I sputtered awkwardly as I felt my face turning red, and like an idiot I said, "No, I, ah... thought you'd be taller." We both laughed, and I wound up having a wonderful hour-long session with one of the most interesting people I have ever met. Most importantly, I learned a valuable lesson about not having preconceived notions.

When he left, I asked myself if the fact that I assumed my friend had married a white man made me a racist. I decided it probably didn't. I'm just human, which equates to being something of an idiot now and then.

Never Try to Out-game a Gamer

I have figured out that when working with people under hypnosis, especially teenagers, it is most effective if I use imagery they can relate to from their business or personal life. This way, my clients are more fully engaged in the process and more likely to recall the information later, when it's needed.

I was working with a teenaged gamer, and I thought I would include some imagery from the video game world. I don't play video games, but my husband does, so I've heard a few things over the years. I thought I'd be cool and use a process where my client could change his feelings about something with the help of a few characters from the video game world.

I brought him out of hypnosis, and the first thing he said was, "Jill, you blew it, a Tauren would not cast that type of spell and would never be friends with a dwarf." I thought I was going to die laughing. Clearly, I was not as cool as I thought. If I wanted to use that kind of imagery, I realized I needed to get it from the teenagers themselves. Better yet, I think I'll stick with what I know!

That's Not Kosher!

My first hypnosis teacher made us memorize a speech to give clients before we begin our sessions, letting them know that while under hypnosis, they could not be compelled to do anything they didn't want to do, and if they were given a suggestion that was against one of their religious beliefs, their mind would likely ignore it, or they would come out of the hypnotic state.

This is one of those things you learn in class, but until you experience it, you don't understand how true it is. I was working with an orthodox Jew on weight loss. She was trying to establish healthier eating habits, both to lose the extra pounds and to increase her health.

While she was hypnotized, I had her imagine the foods she no longer wanted to eat. We completed a process to make those foods less appealing. Next, I listed foods that she should eat more of to maintain a healthier diet. See if you can spot the problem. "Now, see yourself eating lean meats, low-fat dairy products, and…"

I didn't get any further because she suddenly opened her eyes. She didn't actually know why, but I did. Eating meat and milk in the same meal is not considered kosher, especially for an Orthodox Jew. I had blown it, even though I used to work at a Jewish retirement home where we had extensive training on Jewish culture and holidays, especially what was and was not considered kosher! I should've known better! Luckily, as a therapist, I also knew it wouldn't be kosher of me to berate myself too harshly for my mistake.

Chapter 13
It's Always about Healing

A Healer Gets Healed

You'd be surprised at all the good-looking, smart, talented, physically healthy people who have trouble feeling self-assured. This one was a boxer—a huge, scary-looking one at that—whose girlfriend had actually scheduled an appointment on his behalf and revealed that he needed help with his confidence.

He swaggered in, seeming anything but shy, and told me right away he was about to break up with his girlfriend, the one who had scheduled and paid for this visit. He didn't want to talk about their relationship at all.

"Okay," I replied. "What do you want to talk about?" Whether because he knew he wasn't going to see me again, or he just felt like talking, what followed was a refreshingly honest conversation with a man who admitted to something he wasn't proud of.

"I've been to jail a few times for beating up girlfriends. But what I don't understand—and maybe you can explain it to me—is why they stayed with me after I beat them up? Not one of them left. Most of them even bailed me out, and only one actually pressed charges."

I admit I was a bit stunned, but didn't let it show. "Well, this is a hard one to explain completely in a short period of time," I said, "but for some, it's possible you reminded them of someone who abused them before, typically a father figure. This will sound weird, but what is familiar, even if it is bad, is often more comfortable than the unknown… and the unknown could be the experience of a loving, drama-free relationship."

He went on to reveal that many of his girlfriends had admitted to being abused in some way before by a parent, but it wasn't always physical. I explained it didn't have to be, that many are victims of emotional abuse.

"Maybe a few felt, on some level, that if they could figure out how to make you not abuse them, they would heal the earlier harmful relationship. Other women may believe they don't deserve anything better. A truly emotionally healthy person would leave at the first hint of excessive anger, and you wouldn't even get a chance to hit them." This seemed to make sense to him.

I asked him, "Why haven't you sought help for your anger issues? I am sure you've lost some great relationships over it."

He admitted that he had lost some wonderful women, but explained, "I never had any incentive to get help. These girls stayed and believed me when I cried and said I wouldn't do it again. I knew it was bullshit, but they believed it. I think they just wanted to, so they did."

I asked, "If they had walked out after the first time you beat them up, left you in jail and moved out while you were gone, would you have sought help?"

"Probably not after the first time," he told me, "but after the second or third times… yes, for sure, because there would be a consequence. But in my case, there never was. Women have always been easy for me to meet, so when one would leave, I was just on to the next one whom I would hurt, too. I knew what I was doing was wrong, and I wish those women wouldn't have let me get away with it."

After some more talking, I finally said, "I know you don't need help with confidence. So, what would you like to work on with hypnosis?"

"I think my anger problem."

"Excellent choice," I said.

After the session was done, he left, and I never saw him again. However, in our hour together, I had received an amazing gift. You see, very early in my life, I had a boyfriend who was physically abusive, and like this man's girlfriends, I didn't leave right away. Through this client, though, I received something I never had when my relationship ended—his side of the story. While I didn't agree with his actions, I understood why being victimized could have happened to me. Sometimes I wonder if this man came in because there was some aspect of *myself* in need of healing. Regardless of the reason, I am grateful he came to me to talk. It gave me insight and healing closure on an injury from my past.

One of My Most Important Life Lessons

I was seven years old when I learned one of my most important life lessons. My father had taken a job in Hawaii, and the whole family moved from the tiny town of Garfield, Arkansas, to Kailua-Kona, sight unseen. We had been on the island a total of two hours after landing at the airport and obtaining a rental car, when I slammed my hand in the door of our new apartment, cutting off the tip of one of my fingers. We had to take a cab to the hospital because my parents didn't know where it was. I believe I was screaming the whole way.

When we got there, I was introduced to Dr. Kong, an Asian physician who spoke with a very heavy accent. Coming from Arkansas and used to a much different accent, I had a tough time understanding what he was saying. We were told he was a recent immigrant from Vietnam, where he'd headed up the pediatrics department in a hospital there. Now in this country, however, he was unfortunately required to do his residency all over again. We also found out I was one of his first real patients. Getting me, the screaming kid, as his patient was probably part of his dues as "the new guy" at the hospital.

Even though I couldn't quite get what this doctor was saying because he talked funny, when he started calling me "Princess," I understood the universal language of caring. After that point, he got my full attention and most of my cooperation. My finger stopped throbbing after he soaked it in a brown liquid that smelled like iodine.

Dr. Kong gave me a little talk about healing. He started by telling me I was a very lucky little girl, because most people never got to see what the inside of their finger looks like. Using a probe, he showed me what skin tissue looks like from the inside, and then explained how my finger was going to get better.

"You see, Princess, on the surface it looks like I could just tape your finger back on to fix it, but that wouldn't work because the injury is not on the surface. It's deeper down, in places that you can't really see with the eye, and that's where the healing has to start. We will stitch the pieces back together and do things to encourage it to heal, but your body will make it all better from the inside out, not from the outside in."

Much later in my life, it occurred to me that Dr. Kong had been right—real healing does not happen just on the surface, but deep inside and in ways often unseen. The pain itself can't be seen, but the one suffering from it certainly feels its existence.

This describes the fundamental healing of mental illness, which also originates inside us. On the surface, most of the people I work with are fairly healthy. Most have productive lives, are able to pay their bills, and have at least some love in their lives. But they come for help because something in their life isn't working the way they would like it to. This something is what drives them to eat more than they need, feel anxious, sad, and lonely, and then judge themselves negatively because they think they "should" be feeling blissfully happy. They have goals they haven't been able to reach in spite of their best efforts. They sabotage their success, have unsatisfying love relationships, or date the same type of person that hurt them over and over again in the past. They hide how unhappy they really feel from the world by buying nice things and putting on a happy face, but in private they are suffering while stuffing their feelings down with food, alcohol, shopping, and other destructive behaviors. They have fears that keep them from living full and complete lives, keep them from traveling to all the places they want to go, and sometimes even keep them prisoner in their own homes. They long for things they don't think they can have, all the while wishing they could be "normal" without realizing that they are actually the norm. People who are happy all the time, or even most of the time, are the real exceptions.

The people I see come for help because they hope a better life is possible if they fix the kink in their mind. They are on the right track, because many of life's problems start in the mind, and healing must begin where the wounds live.

At the end of my time with my favorite Asian doctor, another physician came up and introduced himself as Dr. Kong's supervisor. He gave my mother home care instructions, as well as a grim warning to have realistic expectations. "Her fingernail will likely fall out and never grow back. The fingertip may never get feeling back, and that whole finger might not ever work completely right. You need to be prepared for that." Dr. Kong taught me another lesson that day about the power of suggestion when he leaned over and whispered in my ear that the other doctor was completely wrong, and that "everything will grow back perfectly and in a year, you won't even be able to tell which one you hurt."

I decided to believe Dr. Kong, and it became so. He was a little off on the timing part, because it took more than a year, but the finger actually healed so well, I would challenge anyone now to figure out which one it was. I also decided that day to become a doctor, although I changed my mind later when my uncle married a doctor, who explained to me what it was really like to work as one. That's a different story, though...

If you decide you want to heal something in your life, take steps toward making this happen. I and others like me have witnessed countless people make extraordinary changes, and we know you can do it. If you're lacking in belief that you can be better, borrow our faith in you until you have your own.

Sudden Mild Depression

When Matt came hobbling into my office on crutches in January, I took one look and said, "Ski accident."

"Yup, Big Bear Mountain," he replied. I already knew he was coming for help with "sudden depression," and just seeing him supplied the reason. I see three or four cases like Matt every ski season, and several others during the rest of the year.

One little-known health fact is that when you take a generally healthy person who is used to getting regular strenuous exercise and suddenly stop them from exercising, they're liable to be hit with a nasty depression. This has to do with the body's chemistry, and the fact many people use exercise as an outlet for stress. When that outlet is gone, normal functioning feels harder, both physically and mentally. Fairly suddenly, life appears to be a cloud-filled challenge with no end in sight.

Most people don't associate an abrupt break from exercise with depression, but they need help in two areas: finding other ways to manage their stress, and coming up with some different way to get physical exercise within their ability. This might consist of such things as tossing a ball around, throwing rolled-up socks at a wall, or lifting free weights from a chair.

My former personal trainer started exercising when her doctor refused to give her a prescription for antidepressants unless she met one condition: "Go to the gym every day for the next thirty days," he instructed her. "If you still need a prescription at the end of thirty days, I'll give you one, but not before." My friend never went back to see him. She found her passion and started a new career instead. In fact, exercise has been clinically shown to be more effective in treating mild depression than any type of antidepressant medication.

Swimming is a good option for many injuries, but always check with your physician, physical therapist, or personal trainer before starting anything new, even if you are wheelchair bound.

When it comes to depression, I always tell people to find a healthy way of coping with it, or else an unhealthy way will find them! The increasing number of housewives and other "atypical" drug addicts who call my office because they "accidentally" became addicted to powerful drugs like oxycodone is a testament to that.

Creative forms of expression including art, meditation, and cooking are additional ways to cope with stress and depression due to a physical injury or for any reason. Many people quickly feel better just learning that their depression is a result of not exercising, because they know this, too, shall pass.

Chapter 14
Odds and Ends

Alien Abductions

Another highly controversial issue within the hypnotherapy community is recollection of alien abductions. Over the years, people have asked about this subject, and every so often a story surfaces about someone who thought they were abducted by aliens and were later able to recall, under hypnosis, details of what the alien beings looked like. The stories they have recounted show a curious degree of consistency. What you don't often hear in the news is that many hypnotherapists seeing people about a supposed alien abduction memory find these patients are actually repressing the memory of a sexual violation.

I discovered this to be true when I had a client come in for what was to be my first suspected alien abduction. This was a man who was aware he had a blocked memory from when he was ten years old and living in a community around people he and his family didn't know. He remembered someone knocking on the door and his opening it. His next recollection after that was a few hours later, when he awoke in his bed feeling like he had been beaten up. Recently in his adulthood, he had seen a TV program about alien abduction, and he thought perhaps this is what had happened to him in that blocked period of time.

During a session, I guided him through a repressed memory process in which I had him open the door to that memory and tell me what he saw. Tragically, what followed was his description of being raped by a male neighbor. As soon as I realized what he was revealing, I took him through another process to release the distress from that memory so it would no longer haunt him. Because neither he nor I was expecting that story, it was disturbing to both of us, and I referred him to a colleague who specializes in sexual violation.

Afterward, I did some research on my own and discovered that sure enough, quite a few hypnotherapists had experienced similar situations with patients who believed they'd been abducted by aliens. I am still curious as to how commonly this occurs.

Sometime later, I saw another female client named Terri, who was convinced she had been abducted by aliens while living in an apartment in New York City. Under hypnosis, what came up was an incident wherein someone had broken into her apartment while she was asleep, held a pillow over her head, and molested but not raped her. This time I was more or less expecting some type of personal violation story, so it wasn't quite as shocking to me. After we finished, Terri asked me a very legitimate question: "Is it possible my mind couldn't handle the idea of an alien abduction and turned it into something I could believe, like someone breaking in? I never saw any evidence of my apartment being broken into ..." I didn't really have an answer for her, except to say, "Sure. That might be possible." The mind can and will do amazing things to cope with unacceptable realities, and there is still much to learn about many of the ways the brain functions for our survival.

Since these two cases, I have stopped seeing clients for alien abduction suspicions. Now I refer these clients to a psychotherapist who knows hypnosis, in the event they have a repressed memory of being violated, in which case a psychotherapist would be the more appropriate choice for treatment. So far, I've never had her tell me that any of these clients had actually been abducted by aliens.

In saying this, it's not my intention to minimize the traumatic event of anyone or rule out that alien abduction does happen. I have lived enough life and witnessed enough strange things to know that nearly anything is possible. Based on my research and experience, however, I feel this phenomenon might best be described as a "close encounter of the *rare* kind."

Awkward Moments

I have kept the weight off.

One day, I was at the gym changing into my swimsuit—basically naked—and a woman I'd never met walked up to me and said, "Aren't you the woman who wrote that book?" She was referring to my weight-loss book, *Feed Your Real Hunger.*

I look a tiny bit like Helen Hunt, and since I am not famous enough to be recognized at the gym, I asked her, "I don't know. Did you like it?"

"Yes, I loved it!" She glanced at my body, and then commented, "And I can see you really have kept the weight off." I was uncomfortable. *This is not my preferred method of proving my weight-loss success*, I thought. But she asked about booking a session, and never one to turn away business, I gave her my card.

She did call to schedule an appointment, and I worked with her for some time on several issues. Strange to think it all started from that very awkward moment in the gym!

I know that guy!

A female client came to me for help in breaking up with her boyfriend, which is a fairly common issue in my practice. She was finding it hard to let him go, even though he was becoming abusive. It showed! She walked into my office with a black eye, and I immediately asked if he had hit her. He had. When I'd booked the appointment, I didn't realize the seriousness and danger of her situation.

It is my policy that if I learn someone I'm treating is currently being physically abused, I refer them to someone I know who specializes in battered woman syndrome (BWS). I always make sure to give the client information on where to get help, and let them know that if they are in danger, they must do so immediately, for their own safety. I spent some time assuring this woman that support was available, and gave her all the resource information she might need, without charging her for my time.

She mentioned the fight had started because she suspected her boyfriend was involved with another woman, and she had confronted him. They hadn't been dating very long, and she had the feeling he might even be married. At that point in our talk, she pulled out a picture of him, and I was stunned. I *knew* him! He was a friend of a friend. He had been to my house, and I knew he was married. I had also always thought he was a really creepy guy; in fact, so much so that I had asked my friend not to bring him over to my house again, as I didn't want his energy in my space.

He had given my client a different name than the one I knew him by, and I was suddenly facing a dilemma. Should I tell her what I knew about him, or let her find things out for herself? I decided to tell her some of what I knew. After all, I had only met him once or twice. I told her what I thought his real name was, but didn't tell her I knew he was married. What if I was wrong, and they had divorced in the past few weeks? I did tell her that it isn't hard to find out if someone is married, and suggested she do some research—research she probably should have done in the beginning of their relationship.

But of course, she was in "looovvee" and had the love blinders on. I've heard it said that love makes you blind. I think that is inaccurate… I think it makes you stupid. You tend to gloss over things you wouldn't ignore if someone were just a friend, such as glaring inconsistencies in their stories.

After receiving assurance from her that she would get additional help, I sent her on her way. A couple weeks later, I received an e-mail thanking me for the referral to the psychotherapist friend of mine who counsels battered women. She let me know she was no longer seeing her boyfriend. "Oh, by the way, I 'Googled' the name you gave me, and wedding pictures came up! He is married … scumbag!" Yup, he sure is.

I'm a sex addict.

Another uncomfortable situation arose when a new client named Joey came into my office looking for help with "confidence issues." I had known Joey before he came in to see me, originally meeting him at a networking event. When he told me the reason he wanted to schedule an appointment with me, I was surprised. He had struck me as quite self-assured.

When he sat down, Joey admitted he wasn't actually there to improve his confidence. The truth was, he had come because he wanted help with sex addiction. I was stunned, and at the time, my first thought was, *If I scream really loud, will anyone else in the building hear me?* This was before Tiger Woods made "sex addiction" more of a household word by stating it was the reason he'd cheated on his wife with so many women. When I met with Joey, I really didn't know much about sex addiction and (incorrectly) assumed I was sitting across from a rapist. This is not true. A sex addict does not necessarily mean the person is a rapist, although some can be.

I referred him elsewhere, since I didn't, and don't, work with that issue. Nonetheless, I still saw him every week for the next two years that I participated in our networking group. Problem was, I could just never get it out of my head that he was a sex addict. There are some things you don't want to know about your colleagues... but once you do, you can't unlearn them.

As a side note, sex addiction is a real issue, and like any addiction, there can be devastating consequences for all those involved. If you or someone you love struggles with this issue, I encourage you to get help for this very serious problem and to read an excellent book on the subject: *Out of the Shadows: Understanding Sexual Addiction* by Patrick Carnes. Like any addiction this is one that truly ruins relationships and whole lives and like other addictions with help it can be treated. If you suffer with this, love yourself and the ones around you enough to get the help you need.

Are you calling my husband a liar?

I got an odd call one day from a woman who identified herself as Maggie. She asked me if I had any appointment options available in the next two weeks. "Yes, I do," I told her. "Are mornings or evenings better for you?"

In a suddenly cold voice, she said, "Then why did you tell my husband you were booked solid for the next three weeks?"

I think I must have made a noise that sounded like "Huh?" because she went on to say that she had told her husband to call me and book an appointment for hypnotherapy. After pestering him a few times, he finally told her he'd made the call, but that I said I was booked solid for the next three weeks.

Now, there are only two situations where I might say that I was booked this fully: (1) I really am booked out for the next three weeks, or (2) the person I am talking to seems creepy and is asking for a late-night appointment. Since as of right now the first situation has never happened, it had to be the second. Still, I hadn't had a creeper-call like that in a long time, so I asked, "Are you sure he called me?"

"Yes," she said curtly. "I am sure. Yours is the only number I gave him." There was a pause, and then in a higher-pitched voice, she said, "Are you saying that my husband lied to me?" (*Yep*, I thought, *basically I am.*) At this point, I couldn't tell if she was angry or really asking me the question, but either way I wanted out of the middle of this, so I asked, "What issue did he want help with?"

"He needs to quit smoking," she replied. After I heard this, it became a bit of a struggle not to laugh because I knew what was going on.

"Is it possible he's not quite ready to quit or just plain doesn't want to?" I remarked.

"It doesn't matter if he's ready or doesn't want to!" Maggie exclaimed. "He must quit because I want him to." Okay, so he didn't call because he doesn't *want* to quit and he wants her off his back... good luck with that.

I knew hypnotherapy wouldn't work if he didn't want it, and I see maybe one smoker per year because it's truly not my favorite thing to work on, so I felt all right in saying, "I am sorry, but I don't really work with people on smoking. If you or he want to work on something else, I would love to see you. For smoking issues, I refer people elsewhere." I then recommended an inexpensive CD series that I know works well for a lot of people. I thought, *At least if he is going to fail, he can do it cheaply and with less frustration.* I never heard from either of them again.

Hypnotherapy is a powerful tool for change, but it's not magic nor will it work if a person doesn't want it to. There is nothing morally wrong with smoking and if this person doesn't want to quit she nor I can make that choice, the choice has to be his. When someone is ready to change, its usually comes fairly easily; when they aren't... well, they lie and tell their wife the hypnotherapist was too busy.

Oh-so-creepy calls.

A man contacted me, asking for help with relationship issues. This is a typical problem area I treat all the time, so I told him I could assist him. The man then made a somewhat random remark about wanting to make sure I wasn't recording our call. Of course, I was not, but I suppose the government does sometimes, so I let him know that if the call was being recorded, it wasn't by me.

He explained that his girlfriend was mad at him because she had heard a story from another woman about something he did at a party. Now, normally at this point, I would go ahead and schedule him because I don't like to hear stories in advance of an actual session, when the issue is our only focus and we can start the healing work while they're talking about it.

But curiosity got the best of me. I asked, "What did she hear?"

"Well, I… uh, it's hard to say, but—" (*Ah, now I really wanted to know!*)

"Well, you see, sometimes when I get really drunk at a party, I have sex with women," he began.

I said, "That sounds like a fairly usual issue of unfaithfulness."

"Umm," he stammered, "I don't always get their consent first … not clear consent, anyway. Sometimes the women are passed out, so I can't ask. I can't seem to stop doing this. Can you help me?"

In my head, I heard my teacher's voice saying, "If you can't see them without judging them, they are not your client." Heck no, this guy wasn't my client! Not only could I not help him, but I didn't want an admitted rapist anywhere near my office.

I told him I couldn't help him, but suggested he find a therapist who specializes in sexual issues. I told him, "I am not saying you are one, but perhaps you might look for someone who works with sex addicts and has experience helping people with what you are describing." After acknowledging him for getting help for his issue and assuring him he was doing the right thing by seeking therapy, I got off the phone and felt like I needed to take a shower. The call had creeped me out. I am sure I have had rapists around me before, as they are among all of us, but there's a huge difference knowing versus not knowing! It's a very uncomfortable awareness, to say the least.

<u>Client with a stalker.</u>

A few years ago, I was working with a client named Lou Ann, who was being stalked by a man named Peter. She had been in a very volatile relationship with him a few years earlier, and it had ended badly. She had moved out, but ever since then, he'd been stalking her. He would show up at parties she attended, hang out near her apartment, and suddenly appear when she was doing ordinary things like going to the mall. She had obtained a restraining order, and because he was violating the California stalking laws, she called the police whenever he showed up. However, he never seemed to spend much time in jail, and his stalking continued.

Lou Ann came to me for help with her feelings of fear for her safety. "I can't sleep at night. I'm constantly looking over my shoulder, afraid."

Unlike others whom I work with on this issue, this woman's fears were real and justified in that they were based on a legitimate threat to her safety.

It just so happens that my brother is a self-defense teacher, and over the years he has given me many lectures on the mental aspects of self-defense, as well as some physical tactics. I worked with Lou Ann on developing the mindset of not being a victim, in addition to strongly recommending she take a self-defense class. I suggested she take the class not necessarily so she could fight back—she swore she never wanted Peter to get close enough to her that she would need these skills—but so that she would feel more physically and emotionally powerful.

As she was leaving one time, she said something that caught my attention: "He seems to always know where I am, and that freaks me out. I don't think he is always following me, so I don't know how he does it."

At one point in my life, my computer had been infected by a variation of the "I Love You" virus, transmitted through an e-card a former boyfriend of mine had sent. The virus installed a program on my computer that allowed him to see what I was doing on my computer, including access to all my e-mails. In my case, it was clear he was deleting e-mails from my box sent by male friends inviting me to social events. At the time, I couldn't figure it out, but knew something strange was going on. The virus was on my computer a long time, and I only found out about it when it caused my computer to crash and my best friend (now my husband, by the way) found it.

I strongly recommended to Lou Ann that she clear her hard drive or even better, get a new laptop, change all her passwords, and consider getting a new phone, e-mail address, and phone number. She said she thought this was overkill, and I figured she might be right until a few days later, when I got a call that felt "off."

It was a man wanting to schedule an appointment at a very specific time, right before my client Lou Ann's appointment two weeks from then. He gave me a very generic-sounding name like John Smith, which I just knew was a lie. At that time, I used PayPal for billing and required my clients to pay when they made their appointment, to ensure they were committed to coming. With PayPal, if the payer had a confirmed merchant account, their name would appear once I typed in their e-mail address to send the invoice. For this guy, Peter's name showed up on my screen! I called him back and let him know I'd been mistaken and didn't actually have that time available, but could see him on a different day. He replied that he could only come that particular day and wasn't interested in any other days or times.

"Sorry, I can't help you," I said, and that was that.

I told Lou Ann about this and again recommended she clear her computer's hard drive. She thanked me, but canceled her next appointment. I haven't heard from her or Peter since. I felt very sorry for her having to deal with this sad and frightening situation, and sincerely hope she found a way to take her life back. Sometimes, overkill isn't overkill, it's being smart. Sneaky people can be amazingly good at finding a way in if they want to. I always tell a client if they feel unsafe there is almost no such thing as overkill. Self-love means valuing yourself enough to do what it takes to be safe. And sometimes that means giving Lenovo some money for a new laptop that's free of spyware.

Odd but Actual

<u>No males allowed.</u>

My client Andrea had been single for many years after her last relationship, which had ended in a relatively usual way. Andrea was well over him, but for some reason she was still uncomfortable getting involved with a new person, and in particular, getting sexually involved or even letting someone stay the night. Since this had never been a problem before, she came to me seeking insight. During our initial discussion, I asked Andrea about the most obvious types of obstacles, including religious issues, feelings of guilt or fear, past sexual traumas, or sadness over loss. However, none of these seemed to be an issue for her.

Finally, I asked Andrea what was going on when her last relationship ended. "That was around the time my dad died, and I had his remains cremated. I still have his ashes, you know," she went on. "I never got around to dumping them at Yosemite, which was his wish."

A light went on in my brain, and I asked, "Where are you storing those ashes?"

"In my bedroom on the mantle," she revealed. "It helps me think about him every day."

"So Andrea, are you saying your dad is in your bedroom all the time?"

"Yes, and I really feel his presence."

I considered for a moment and then said, "Hmm… do you think that may not exactly be a turn-on for you sexually?"

Andrea laughed and said she had never thought of that. Finally she agreed that this might be the problem.

As it turned out, with her dead father literally sleeping in her bedroom, it was hard for her to get excited about having a man over. Not long after his ashes made it to Yosemite, Andrea was able to get into a new relationship with a wonderful man. Sometimes the solution to our issue is not obvious, and we can easily overlook simple causes of what appear to be complicated issues.

No end to no sleep.

One of my clients suffered severe sleep issues, and while she explored with her doctor the idea that there might be a physical component to her difficulties, I tried to help her look at the emotional upsets that might be causing her to wake up frequently in the night. After several sessions with her, she said her sleeping had improved somewhat, but she still some fitful nights. I was getting a bit frustrated because this is usually a pretty quick fix. I felt we weren't really getting to the heart of this, and I kept wondering what we were missing. At the end of her third session, as she was leaving, she remarked, "I wonder if this could have anything to do with the fact that my mom used to sleep in my bed with me?"

Probably most mothers sleep with their children at one point or another, but not everyone has sleep issues. Therefore, at first I doubted this could be related until I asked her, "How often did she do this?"

My client replied, "Every night from when I was a baby to when I went off to college at eighteen. I think she was trying to avoid having to have sex with my dad, who would frequently come in and try to get her to sleep with him. She didn't want to, though."

What?! Right away I said, "Yes… that might have something to do with it!" We started working on that part of the problem, and not long after I started noticing this was a pattern with other sleep clients. When client's parents slept with them long into teen years the adult seems to have a lot of trouble getting to sleep alone. I wish parents wouldn't do this late into the teen years since it seems to cause real problems later on in life.

Sometimes the best information I get from clients comes as they are getting up and ready to leave, and offhandedly remark, "I wonder if this could have anything to do with…?" As a healing practitioner, I've learned to pay close attention to these last few words patients say after they have just been hypnotized, and they are still more in tune with their unconscious mind. It's surprising how valuable that information can be. I don't know how many times I've taken a frantic note about what we need to work on next time from something a client mentioned as they were walking out the door!

"One Jedi Mind Trick, Please"

My Tuesday 10:00 a.m. appointment was with one of my favorite clients, Zachary. The reason I liked to see him was not because he was particularly nice or funny—actually, he was neither of these—and on the contrary, he could be pretty annoying at times. However, he was fun because he challenged my mind! He worked locally as a programmer, and he was a huge *Star Wars* fan. He never disappointed me in coming up with some crazy Jedi mind trick request that usually sent me straight to Google afterward to see if what he wanted was even possible. Although supposedly coming to me for confidence issues, which he certainly had, I nevertheless suspected he just thought hypnosis was cool and was hoping to learn a new trick.

As usual, Zachary was in good form. "I just saw *Ghost Hunters* last night [actually, one of my favorite shows, too] and they talked about something called 'sleep paralysis,' where your body paralyzes itself during sleep so that you don't do something harmful to yourself, like biting off your own tongue." Yep, I'd seen that episode.

Next came his request: "Okay, so I want you to hypnotize me so deep that it triggers sleep paralysis, only I want to be able to open my eyes and look around."

With Zachary, my first question—once I think I can open my mouth without laughing—is usually "Why?"

"I dunno," he said today. "I think it would be cool to have that much control, plus I could probably freak out my buddies with it."

On one of our previous sessions, Zachary had come in with a real gem—asking me if I could hypnotize someone to make them kill another person. He'd said, "Jill, you told me on our first session that it wasn't possible, but I saw this YouTube video where someone proved you could do it. So I think you're wrong!"

"First," I told him, "I also saw that video and still think it wouldn't work in reality, but I will amend my earlier statement to say I don't *think* it can be done, and I certainly didn't learn any hypnosis techniques to make someone do that. So we'll just leave it at that, okay?"

But back to the sleep paralysis thing… this time I knew something bizarre would be presented by Zachary, so my laptop was already on the site I often use to look up the weird things he comes up with. I said, "I'm pretty sure that's not possible, but let's just do a quick check." I already know he's probably Googled this himself and found the same information I have access to, but he's testing me. Since both of us actually enjoy this game, I don't mind playing along.

"Nope," I told him after checking it out. According to Wikipedia, it's only possible during the transitional state between sleeping and waking, a state we only drift through. During hypnosis, the client hovers in a lighter state of consciousness to do our work and then moves back into regular awareness. "Not possible," I continued. "Anything else you want to know while I have my laptop open?"

Zachary was disappointed. "But why?" he said in his particularly whiny voice that sounded like it was coming from a twelve-year-old, a tone I was used to hearing whenever I told him "no."

Although Zachary was very confident in many areas of his life, he found it very difficult asking a woman out on a date, speaking to women in general, and even chatting with them at a party. He never said this directly, but I think he came to me hoping that, in addition to helping him with confidence, I could teach him a new, cool trick that might make it easier for him to talk to women.

I see a lot of engineers like Zachary… really nice guys, great catches, but often painfully shy and socially awkward. These are the real forty-year-old virgins. In a practice full of women who met, dated, and married outgoing, smooth-talking pick-up artists who never gave up their "player" ways and turned out to be not-so-great husbands, I find it very sad that more women don't take the risk to ask these engineer-types out. They work hard, are generally pretty loyal companions, and what I hear over and over from them is that just like most guys, they are looking for someone special to settle down with, "or just any woman, at this point," as Zachary put it one time.

My client was not unattractive, but somewhat inept socially, even by my very liberal standards. He would ask questions about politics and say slightly inappropriate things that were somewhat off-putting if you didn't already know him. Zachary would come to my office in a stained Star Trek t-shirt he'd gotten at Comic-Con the year before. He needed a haircut and contacts, and could use some wardrobe help, but much of what needed to be said to him was better coming from another man than from me.

Zachary, who was in no way flirtatious, told me once, "You smell nice." I had to tell him that although that sounded like a nice thing to say, it might seem too personal to a woman he didn't know well.

"Then why wear perfume if you don't want someone to say something?" he asked, in a way that told me he was sincerely curious and not offended by what I had said.

"Honestly," I replied, "I don't exactly know why it seems creepy… it just does. And while we're on the subject, don't ask women out on a date at the gym [he had recently been shot down by a married woman who was not wearing her wedding ring at the gym]. When we are in gym clothes, we feel vulnerable, and that doesn't make us as open to being approached."

Of course, Zachary had more questions. "But why do women go to the gym in full makeup if they don't want to be approached?"

"Probably because they are at the gym before or after work," I reasoned. "It's not because they want a date, though. You need to approach women where they feel comfortable, like at a coffee house, at work, or at church." The problem with this advice was that Zachary didn't go to church, and in a male-dominated field, almost all of his coworkers were men ("except the marketing women, and they are almost all former models and not approachable"). Although I hate to say it, the preponderance of males at most technology companies is a reality. I feel for these young, single programmers.

With Zachary, I always had this secret thought that he wanted to be a superhero with special powers. What he didn't understand was that he already did have special powers! The company he programmed for makes medical devices that save lives. When I went to the emergency room for appendicitis, I was hooked up to one of his company's machines, one he worked on. And although his job isn't sexy, it's probably contributed to saving more lives than what most people do all day—my own job included. Zachary knew several programming languages and had the ability to focus deeply on complex problems for hours at a time without stopping, which is a *real* Jedi mind trick.

Engineers in general seem to complain about lack of confidence most frequently, and yet at the same time, are among the most intelligent of anyone I see. In spite of their exceptional abilities, they tend to focus on the fact that they have trouble asking someone out on a date. This unfortunate lack of social confidence, I suspect, keeps many of the world's most capable humans from reaching their full potential.

In fact, as human beings, we often don't see the value of what we do because we miss the bigger picture. Everyone has unique gifts, although the people who have them don't always derive feelings of self-esteem from these talents. We need our engineers to be cerebral and build our bridges, need our extroverted salespeople (or more commonly these days, introverted salespeople) to go out and motivate people to want to pay for that bridge using their talent of explaining why we need strong bridges and why it's worth paying more money to build them. We need the quiet accountants to ensure that everyone and everything gets paid, and the assistants and secretarial support staff to make sure everyone gets what they need to do their jobs efficiently and effectively.

The bottom line is that everyone is really important, and my role is sometimes to help people see how what they do is vital in the operation of the world as a whole. Maybe that's *my* Jedi mind trick.

What's yours?

Alternative Sexual Lifestyles—Really?

I used to believe that people who engaged in three-way sex, or were participants in sex clubs, polyamory, or "swinging," must have some really messed-up emotional issues, and that this behavior was a symptom. Since working with clients doing all of the above, however, I'm not so sure anymore.

Although talking to people who engage in alternative sexual lifestyles is not an everyday occurrence in my practice, especially since I don't work with clients on specific sexual issues, I run across it far more than I expected.

As it turns out, in San Diego there is a large polyamory community. Polyamory—not to be confused with polygamy, in which a man has more than one "wife"—refers to a man and woman engaged in a primary relationship (a "marriage") while both also participate in sexual activity with others. Over the years, I've come across a great number of clients who belong to sex or swinger's clubs, or are part of long-term sexual relationships with more than one person, which is similar to a marriage, only with three people involved instead of two.

With the exception of polygamy, which I personally find abusive toward women, I found myself having to rethink the conventional wisdom I'd been taught, because aside from their sexual choices, these clients' issues were pretty typical and in line with what I was used to seeing in my practice.

Such was the case with my client Sandra, who came to me to address jealousy issues she was having with her husband. They were part of a sex club or group (I never got clear which it was) that engaged in swinger's activities. She and her husband would have sex with other people, often at the same time and sometimes in the same bed, on a fairly routine basis. Sandra said she found it to be quite a turn-on to watch her husband having sex with another woman. The problem was that she was now feeling jealous because she saw some texts and e-mails sent between her husband and one of these women.

I was pretty stupefied. I asked, "So let me get this straight… you are completely okay with your husband having sex with other women—"

"I am not just okay with it," she interrupted. "I like it. It's fun to watch."

"Okay. Thank you for being clear with me. So, you are okay with sex, but not with other outside communication like texts, e-mails, and phone calls."

Sandra nodded. "Yes! I'm upset with both him and that other woman for not following the rules. As a couple, my husband and I do not have hidden contact with the other people we play with. We are both allowed to send e-mails and the like, but the conversation has to include all three of us so it's not a secret. They have been sending texts and not including me."

Whenever I have worked with people who practice alternative sexual activities, I always hear a lot about the "rules of engagement." With regular couples, the rules are fairly simple, starting with "no sexual activity outside of the relationship." Also, there is usually another restriction against becoming strongly emotionally involved with another person who could be a potential threat to the relationship. With my alternative lifestyle clients, the rules are somewhat different and much more spelled out. I think making the boundaries very clear actually works better within the playing field of this lifestyle, probably absolutely essential for it to work.

In Sandra's case, her husband, Barry, and the other woman, Abby, had been continuing the relationship outside the rules of engagement, and this naturally wasn't going over well. "When I confronted him," she said, "he got upset. He doesn't understand why I would be jealous because he forgot to copy me on the texts and told me, 'After all, we're just talking.' He showed me all the texts and it's nothing very interesting, but I don't like it. I admit, he's done this before and it didn't really bother me then, but for some reason now it does and I'm not sure why. Barry says it's *my* problem because I was cheated on in the past, and he said I need therapy."

I had a couple thoughts about what Sandra told me. First, when someone doesn't follow the rules within a relationship, and then, rather than realize their mistake and apologize, they come back with, "If that bothers you, it's your problem," it's hard to feel like you can really trust them.

I explained to her, "Yes, perhaps it's true you could use some more healing work on leftover trust issues from being cheated on in the past, but you are not making up the fact he's doing something against the rules."

Second, it is often the case with couples that when one person in the relationship is not getting their needs met, they will start to fixate on things that ordinarily wouldn't bother them much at all. This is very typical of any client, regardless of conventional or unconventional sexual lifestyle. I asked Sandra how the relationship was going otherwise, and she let me know that Barry was on a new, very intense project at his job and had been working late frequently over the last few months. As a result, she felt lonely and was missing the quality time together they used to spend doing ordinary things like watching television and going to the gym.

She didn't think Barry was cheating on her, and what she told me seemed to make sense. "Why would he need to? We already have sex outside of our relationship, so there is no need to do that. He's just really busy, and that's not going to change for at least the next six months." She went on, "I feel like when he sends her texts or e-mails, he is taking away from the limited time or conversation that we could be having, and that bothers me." Although Sandra understood that texts don't take long to send, she wished he sent more to her and not someone else.

I suggested she talk to Barry about her feelings and ask for more texts, e-mails, and quality time together, but I also strongly recommended she find something for herself to focus on besides him and their relationship. With his being unavailable at present, it would be a good time for her to get busy. I suggested, "It might be time to take that pottery class you thought would be fun, or start that side business, or write that book you've been thinking about writing."

I also recommended marriage counseling if she felt they needed it, which is a suggestion I give everyone who comes in with these types of issues, regardless of their sexual choices/lifestyles.

Actually, Sandra and Barry's problem is something I've heard variations of about once a week since I started practicing. Working with Sandra made me realize, however, that no matter how different people might seem in certain ways, their feelings and conflicts are the same. Furthermore, Barry and Sandra, though not unattractive, definitely didn't look like super-endowed porn stars, as people might imagine. The experience was a real eye-opener to me and a good lesson about not judging people based only on one aspect of their lives, especially something I don't completely understand.

Accepting that everyone's version of "normal" is up to them means that the same way we defend our lifestyle choices, we shouldn't judge or condemn others' choices, so long as they aren't affecting us or our quality of life. If more people thought outside the box they've been socialized in, think how much stronger and more peaceful our world might be.

The Heartbreakingly Easy Problem to Solve

One of the most difficult parts of being a practitioner is seeing a client fail. When I say "fail," I'm not talking about the client not reaching their goal, as in not losing the amount of weight they wanted to lose or achieving the result they wanted. I don't consider these situations as failures, but rather as part of learning and sometimes adjusting the approach used.

Failure to me is when a client cannot or will not see the value of investing the time, expense, and work it takes to create lasting healing for themselves. They apparently don't understand that they are worth the effort it takes to heal, whether to change their weight/body size or shed destructive habits and attitudes. Sadly, this happens all the time.

One example was when Trish, a prospective client, contacted me because of a challenging yet totally solvable problem. She was having trouble staying connected in a long-distance relationship, and she also suffered extreme separation anxiety. Whenever her boyfriend would leave, an intense sadness would come over her, along with the fear that she would never see him again. This made her very clingy with him when he had to go somewhere, and she would insist they schedule their next date right then and there to allay her anxiety. Basically, Trish said she was a "wreck" whenever her boyfriend went away.

Knowing how difficult this issue can be, and how destructively those feelings can affect anyone's quality of life, I was happy that Trish contacted me, because I knew I could help her. Her problem is actually one of the easier issues to resolve using the tool of hypnosis, and I knew Trish would feel a lot better even after just one session.

After scheduling an appointment with Trish, my mind was already busy planning out her protocol, anticipating some of the conversation, and feeling happy knowing she would see improvement very quickly. I could see the light at the end of her tunnel of pain, and it wasn't an idiot holding a match!

Unfortunately, Trish never made it in for help. At her appointment time, she called me complaining that I didn't "warn her" about San Diego traffic (doesn't everyone who *drives* know there may be traffic?), that she would arrive too late at this point, and that all of this was *my* fault. She then added that she thought I charged too much, my intake forms were too long, and a couple of other silly, untrue "reasons" why she wouldn't/couldn't come. In spite of all her angry justification, I knew that probably because of the same issues that caused her trouble in the first place, Trish was backing away from her own healing. I was sure she did this in many areas of her life—blaming others for her problems, complaining about the cost of things, and probably not taking any help or advice offered that could really help her. Maybe she and I weren't a match for treatment, but our conversation told me that on some level, she wasn't ready. Trish canceled her appointment and never called again.

It made me a bit sad, as it always does when this type of thing happens in my practice, that Trish was one more person in the world suffering needlessly and at her own hands. Her pain doubtlessly affected those around her, too … her friends, coworkers, the family watching her suffer, and maybe even a person she cut off on the freeway because her anger toward her boyfriend turned into road rage. Her boyfriend was likely the most affected, and whether or not they were a good match for each other, it was almost a guarantee that their relationship was already, or certainly would be, sorely tested by her issues.

I've talked with many practitioners about people flaking out on their own healing, and not surprisingly, it's a very common drawback in the therapy field. Patients either stop showing up for the appointments they make for themselves or stop treatment too early when there is still a lot more work to do. Sometimes they say they can't afford treatment, which is always a ready excuse. My experience over the years, however, is that when people are ready to heal, they find a way to make it happen no matter what, even if that means sacrificing some material comfort for a short time, finding child care, or rearranging their schedule so they can keep their appointments. For those who are not ready, any excuse to cancel is used, and if none is available, the inner saboteur creates one.

Our egos hate change, and will fight like heck to keep the status quo, even if it's a lousy one. Change—even beneficial change—can be hard because it requires us to grow, shift, and create different habits around the new way of being. Even if something isn't good, such as being in a bad relationship, there is a certain degree of comfort in it because it's familiar.

I have to face this with clients all the time and it stings, not so much because of loss of business—although I love what I do and being busy—but because I know that society at large is made better when someone gets healed. The reverse is also unfortunately true.

If you only get one thing from this book, I hope it is this: Don't give up on yourself. Don't let money, your or your kids' schedules, "life," or whatever obstacle you run across, keep you from the quality of living you deserve. Life goes on whether you are healthy and whole or not, so you may as well get healed! If you consider what you spend your money on, why *wouldn't* you pay to get help for the most important person in your and your loved ones' world—you?

There are few things in this world that can't be made better through creative solutions. Your physical, emotional, and spiritual health are the most important things to attend to, for your own benefit and that of this world we all share. Remember that no matter how things may "seem" at any given moment, you are loved, special, and extremely important! There is something on this planet that you, and *only* you, can do. Value yourself enough to heal the wounds that block you from sharing your unique contribution.

In the End, It's All about Love

One of my teachers specialized in working with drug addicts. She told us she didn't start off intending to do this. One person come to her with this problem looking for help, and they worked so well together that he wound up sending his friends, who sent their friends, and so on.

This teacher clearly had an ability to connect with addicts in a way that I didn't, so one day in class I asked her about it. She said, "My father died of a drug overdose, so I understand the impact of using drugs on the lives of those around the addict. Mostly, though, I think they are able to understand that I love them."

That seemed like an odd answer, so I asked her to explain this a bit more. "My clients know that no matter what they do, whom they stole from or slept with for drugs, I love them and won't judge them for what they did. That's not my job. What you have to understand is that for some of these people, feeling like someone loves them and cares if they live or die is an experience they haven't felt in a while, if at all. I've had clients tell me that they were about to use, but saw my face in their mind and didn't want to disappoint me, so they put the needle down."

I could relate to this, since that's what I liked about her, too—even though her teaching style was kind of intense sometimes, I knew that underneath this, she cared about me and the others in the class and truly wanted us to be the best we could be. Her motivation to make us great at what we did was not so that we'd make more money—although this might be a result—but because being better practitioners and people in general would fulfill us, and society would benefit from our stronger abilities to heal others.

Every day in my business, I strive to convey that no matter what, I care about my clients and want them to succeed. Sometimes that means saying "no," setting boundaries about being on time, letting me know twenty-four hours in advance about rescheduling, and paying before the session so I know they are committed to coming. I don't set these boundaries just for me, although I admit I wouldn't do this business if I didn't have them in place. I do this because I know clients who keep those sacred appointments they make with and for themselves get better, and those who don't, make no progress.

I'm not going to lie and imply that all the clients I see find the success they're looking for, but I never fail to try to make that happen. This is because at my very core, I care about people and I know that everyone has amazing potential, much of it unrealized, and I hate to see each person's unique potential go to waste because of fear, lack of confidence (fear again), anxiety (mostly fear), and limiting beliefs adopted somewhere along the line that hold them back (mostly created because of fear).

I have had to say to clients, "If you don't show up for your appointments with yourself that take place in my office, I can't help you get better. I want you to get better because I care about you and the impact these problems have on your life and the lives of your families." They don't always like hearing this, but I wouldn't feel right if I didn't honestly convey to them how important it is that they do the actual work of healing so they can have success.

Even if you don't have children of your own, there is someone in your life, maybe even several people, who look up to you or turn to you for guidance and support. Try every day in some manner to convey to them that you love them. To do this, words aren't always appropriate, as in the case of someone at your job, which could be awkward; however, communicating that they matter to you and you want them to succeed can be done with actions, also. Setting boundaries or rules for your interaction with each other is one unspoken way you treat yourself and them with love, because these things will help them move forward. It's all about love, beginning with loving yourself, and thereby learning how to better love those around you.

My Lunch Date with a Cop
and the Reason I Wrote This Book

Several years ago while my practice was still new, I was at a self-help seminar in LA... being a bit of a junkie for this type of thing, I can't even tell you which one it was. Around noon, our instructor told us to go to lunch with the *last* person in the room whom you would normally spend time with.

I spotted my guy right away, a very large African American man with tattoos all over his arms, and pairing with him seemed inevitable as he was walking right toward me. I asked, "Are you my lunch date?" to which he replied, "It would seem so, ma am." "Great! You drive, I'll pay," I said. What followed was one of the most interesting and enlightening noon breaks I have ever had.

It turned out that my new acquaintance was a cop who worked vice, frequently undercover, and as such, spent much of his time with people the rest of us would never want to be around. One of the main differences between us popped out right away when he mentioned that he was armed at all times.

"What?" I gawked. "Even now, at a self-help seminar?" Stunned, I hoped he wasn't about to show me his gun!

"Yes, at all times. What I do is dangerous, and I want to be prepared."

I never, ever intend to have a job where I need to be armed at all times as a basic precaution, so I could see right away that we lived very different lives in some fundamental ways. Regardless of this, it was our similarities, not our differences, that struck me the most after our lunch together.

We were both products of a violent home life at the hands of our fathers, from whom our mothers failed to protect us. We both had decided early on that the cycle of violence in our families was going to end with us, which is why we had signed up for self-help classes. We were both trying to make ourselves healthier people so we could create better futures for us and any family we might have.

The policeman even explained that his tattoos were art and that each one had meaning to him. Looking at them more closely, I realized that they really were quite beautiful.

My lunch date turned out to be a very interesting person, and I'm so glad I had the opportunity to spend time with him. It occurred to me that in the "real world," we wouldn't likely have met unless something bad had happened and I'd needed to call the police for help. That seemed kind of sad.

In thinking about this, I also concluded that people in general don't spend enough time with others who are different from themselves. I don't only mean different races, but different religions, lifestyles, sexual orientations, and nationalities. We don't get the opportunities to hear others' stories, share in their experiences, and learn by seeing how they do things. We miss out on all the new input and perspectives we might gain from reaching outside our comfort zone.

On the way back to class, we happened to be driving through Brentwood, so my companion asked if I wanted to see the house where Nicole Brown Simpson had been killed. He knew where it was. I said, "Hmm. Something creepy and morbid, that might be haunted? Heck yeah!!" Oddly enough, on the drive over there, we were pulled over by a patrolman for what appeared to be no reason. While one of the officers talked to my date, the other came to my side of the car and asked if I was okay. Perplexed I asked, "Why wouldn't I be, do you know something I don't?" He didn't answer, and they let us go pretty quickly and without much discussion when they found out they were dealing with a fellow cop.

Heading back to class, there was silence in the car. I broke in saying, "I'm sorry."

"For what?" he asked me. "You didn't do anything." More silence, and then, "Don't worry about it. That happens all the time."

"That's why I'm sorry," I told him. "Because that never happens to me."

I don't pretend to know what it's like to be an African American, or a police officer doing a dangerous job for ridiculously low pay, but that lack of comprehension is what happens when we limit our interactions to people just like us. Acceptance of others' differences can only come through communicating with them. It's hard to dislike someone you understand, even if you don't agree with them.

It may be more than a little weird to ask someone very dissimilar from you out to lunch, but if you can, I hope the experience will be as hugely rewarding and enlightening as mine was. That one lunch date of mine changed my view of the world and people forever—a little empathy goes a long way in creating peace among us.

This incident is the reason I wrote this book. I was hoping to shed light on the lives and lifestyles of people who may be different from you. I have worked with police officers, prostitutes, homemakers, programmers, church deacons, and just about everything in between, and I have learned a great deal from those people. My hope is that you see that at the end of the day that we really aren't that different from each other.

Day in and day out I hear from clients with issues I see all the time, expressing how alone they feel in their struggles and how they feel like they are the only one. They are sometimes surprised when I say "you are unique but your problem isn't, many people have that issue and it can be resolved." I also wish that people are able to see that we aren't so different after all. We all feel that we are faking it, that we have difficult relationship issues, and that we have fears we don't understand.

As human beings, we are all connected by our desire to love, to be loved, and to feel connected. And it is that among other things that makes us all the same.

If I could have one wish for something I would like you, the reader, to get from this book, it is that you are important. You are worth healing, and no matter how difficult your struggles are they can be resolved. You have something very important and very special to share with the world. Please don't let your light be diminished by anything or allow anyone else to make you feel small. You aren't.

I love you all and thank you so much for letting me share these stories with you in the spirit of connection.

One last thing for my fellow healers and healers-to-be: know that we are all in this together and that you are loved, supported, and valued for your efforts regardless of what the world (or your boss, if you're working for others) might say! Don't ever forget that.

To all of you, I wish you limitless love. Thank you for reading.

Acknowledgments

I must thank my amazing editor and friend, Christine Miller, who believed in this project wholeheartedly and helped me feel confident about its success. I also thank my favorite hypnotherapy teacher, Michele Meiche, whose tireless love and support helped me to be both a better hypnotherapist and a better person; and my intuition and channeling teacher, Lori Camacho, whose love, support, and dedication to my growth helped me be a better intuitive and channel than I ever thought possible. To Ki's restaurant in Encinitas, who tolerated my hours of sitting there sipping coffee and writing, thank you. In fact, I wrote so much of this book there that I really should give them royalties, but I won't, so I hope they will accept this instead. Thank you to my amazing clients whose lives I was allowed to be a part of while they shared their joys, sorrows, and even their defeats with me. For that I am truly honored.

About the Author

Jill K. Thomas, CHT, is a Board-certified hypnotherapist, author, clairvoyant, medium, and channel, who has devoted her life's work to helping anyone whose issues limit their personal freedom and happiness. She has appeared on numerous radio shows, maintains her popular online blog, "Confessions of a Hypnotherapist," and has authored articles for magazines read across the nation. In 2012, Jill wrote and published *Feed Your Real Hunger: Getting off the Emotional Treadmill that Keeps You Overweight* (www.feedyourrealhunger.com), an invaluable guide for individuals trying to lose weight by utilizing self-hypnosis techniques to confront and change core beliefs that bind them to the battle with overeating and negative body image.

In *Tales from the Trance*, Jill's first work with Ozark Mountain Publishing, she expands her expert discussion beyond just weight loss to the vast scope of human struggles keeping so many trapped and unable to progress in life. Years of assisting clients through hypnotherapy and her natural psychic abilities have afforded Jill a wealth of experience and success stories to share.

Jill lives in Encinitas, California with her husband and more cats than she cares to admit! For more information, or to sign up for her blog visit: www.soulconnecthypnotherapy.com

If you liked this book, you might also like:

Dance of Eternal Rapture
by Garnet Schulhauser

Between Death & Life
by Dolores Cannon

The Anne Dialogues
by Guy Needler

A Funny Thing Happen on the Way to Heaven
by Grant Pealer

The Dawn Book
by Annie Stillwater Gray

Not Your Average Angel Book
by Andy Myers

Baby It's You
by Maureen McGill

For more information about any of the above titles, soon to be released titles,
or other items in our catalog, write, phone or visit our website:
Ozark Mountain Publishing, Inc.
PO Box 754, Huntsville, AR 72740
479-738-2348
www.ozarkmt.com

For more information about any of the titles published by Ozark Mountain Publishing, Inc., soon to be released titles, or other items in our catalog, write, phone or visit our website:

Ozark Mountain Publishing, Inc.

PO Box 754

Huntsville, AR 72740

479-738-2348/800-935-0045

www.ozarkmt.com

Other Books by Ozark Mountain Publishing, Inc.

Dolores Cannon
A Soul Remembers Hiroshima
Between Death and Life
Conversations with Nostradamus,
    Volume I, II, III
The Convoluted Universe -Book One,
    Two, Three, Four, Five
The Custodians
Five Lives Remembered
Jesus and the Essenes
Keepers of the Garden
Legacy from the Stars
The Legend of Starcrash
The Search for Hidden Sacred Knowledge
They Walked with Jesus
The Three Waves of Volunteers and the
    New Earth
Aron Abrahamsen
Holiday in Heaven
Out of the Archives – Earth Changes
Justine Alessi & M. E. McMillan
Rebirth of the Oracle
Kathryn/Patrick Andries
Naked in Public
Kathryn Andries
The Big Desire
Dream Doctor
Soul Choices: Six Paths to Find Your Life
    Purpose
Soul Choices: Six Paths to Fulfilling
    Relationships
Patrick Andries
Owners Manual for the Mind
Dan Bird
Finding Your Way in the Spiritual Age
Waking Up in the Spiritual Age
Julia Cannon
Soul Speak – The Language of Your Body
Ronald Chapman
Seeing True
Albert Cheung
The Emperor's Stargate
Jack Churchward
Lifting the Veil on the Lost Continent of
    Mu
The Stone Tablets of Mu
Sherri Cortland
Guide Group Fridays

Raising Our Vibrations for the New Age
Spiritual Tool Box
Windows of Opportunity
Cinnamon Crow
Chakra Zodiac Healing Oracle
Teen Oracle
Patrick De Haan
The Alien Handbook
Paulinne Delcour-Min
Spiritual Gold
Michael Dennis
Morning Coffee with God
God's Many Mansions
Arun & Sunanda Gandhi
The Forgotten Woman
Carolyn Greer Daly
Opening to Fullness of Spirit
Anita Holmes
Twidders
Victoria Hunt
Kiss the Wind
Diane Lewis
From Psychic to Soul
Donna Lynn
From Fear to Love
Maureen McGill
Baby It's You
Maureen McGill & Nola Davis
Live from the Other Side
Curt Melliger
Heaven Here on Earth
Henry Michaelson
And Jesus Said – A Conversation
Dennis Milner
Kosmos
Andy Myers
Not Your Average Angel Book
Guy Needler
Avoiding Karma
Beyond the Source – Book 1, Book 2
The Anne Dialogues
The History of God
The Origin Speaks
James Nussbaumer
And Then I Knew My Abundance
The Master of Everything
Mastering Your Own Spiritual Freedom

For more information about any of the above titles, soon to be released titles,
or other items in our catalog, write, phone or visit our website:
PO Box 754, Huntsville, AR 72740
479-738-2348/800-935-0045
www.ozarkmt.com

Other Books by Ozark Mountain Publishing, Inc.

Sherry O'Brian
Peaks and Valleys
Riet Okken
The Liberating Power of Emotions
Gabrielle Orr
Akashic Records: One True Love
Let Miracles Happen
Victor Parachin
Sit a Bit
Nikki Pattillo
A Spiritual Evolution
Children of the Stars
Rev. Grant H. Pealer
A Funny Thing Happened on the
Way to Heaven
Worlds Beyond Death
Victoria Pendragon
Born Healers
Feng Shui from the Inside, Out
Sleep Magic
The Sleeping Phoenix
Michael Perlin
Fantastic Adventures in Metaphysics
Walter Pullen
Evolution of the Spirit
Debra Rayburn
Let's Get Natural with Herbs
Charmian Redwood
A New Earth Rising
Coming Home to Lemuria
David Rivinus
Always Dreaming
Richard Rowe
Imagining the Unimaginable
M. Don Schorn
Elder Gods of Antiquity
Legacy of the Elder Gods
Gardens of the Elder Gods
Reincarnation...Stepping Stones of Life

Garnet Schulhauser
Dance of Eternal Rapture
Dance of Heavenly Bliss
Dancing Forever with Spirit
Dancing on a Stamp
Annie Stillwater Gray
Education of a Guardian Angel
The Dawn Book
Work of a Guardian Angel
Blair Styra
Don't Change the Channel
Natalie Sudman
Application of Impossible Things
L.R. Sumpter
The Old is New
We Are the Creators
Jim Thomas
Tales from the Trance
Janie Wells
Embracing the Human Journey
Payment for Passage
Dennis Wheatley/ Maria Wheatley
The Essential Dowsing Guide
Maria Wheatley
Druidic Soul Star Astrology
Jacquelyn Wiersma
The Zodiac Recipe
Sherry Wilde
The Forgotten Promise
Lyn Willmoth
A Small Book of Comfort
Stuart Wilson & Joanna Prentis
Atlantis and the New Consciousness
Beyond Limitations
The Essenes -Children of the Light
The Magdalene Version
Power of the Magdalene
Robert Winterhalter
The Healing Christ

For more information about any of the above titles, soon to be released titles,
or other items in our catalog, write, phone or visit our website:
PO Box 754, Huntsville, AR 72740
479-738-2348/800-935-0045
www.ozarkmt.com